STRANGE DEFEAT

Strange Defeat

A STATEMENT OF EVIDENCE
WRITTEN IN 1940

BY
MARC BLOCH

With an Introduction by
SIR MAURICE POWICKE

And a Foreword by
GEORGES ALTMAN

Translated from the French
by
GERARD HOPKINS

W. W. NORTON & COMPANY
New York • London

First published as a Norton paperback 1968 by
arrangement with Oxford University Press; reissued 1999

ISBN: 978-0-393-31911-8

W. W. Norton & Company, Inc., 500 Fifth Avenue, New York, N.Y. 10110
www.wwnorton.com

W. W. Norton & Company, Ltd., 15 Carlisle Street, London W1D 3BS

4 5 6 7 8 9 0

Contents

Introduction

THIS penetrating, poignant, outspoken book stands out among other books about France and the first year of the Second World War as the work of a very distinguished scholar, a professor of the Sorbonne, who was later to be one of the leaders in the movement of resistance and to be put to death for his part in it. The book is a piece of analysis and a contemporary judgement by a man who wrote as a Frenchman, 'that is to say, a civilized man, for the two are identical', but also, and always, as a French historian who had earned the right to be heard.

Marc Bloch began his career as a writer and teacher of history in 1905, in his twentieth year. His family was firmly established in France. He tells us that a great-grandfather fought in the revolutionary army in 1793, that his father fought in 1870. He himself fought in the First World War and, at the age of fifty-three, the father of six children, was again in service in 1939; but he wrote this book as a student of history. The turning-point in his academic life came, I think, in 1929, the year in which he gave a course of lectures at Oslo on the invitation of the Norwegian Institute for the Comparative Study of Institutions, for these lectures gave rise to his finest book, *Les Caractères originaux de l'histoire rurale française*; and it was in the same year that, with M. Lucien Febvre, he founded the *Annales d'histoire économique et sociale*, the periodical which he used as a forum, and through which he became one of the most influential economic and social historians of his time. During the years after the First World War he had tended to concentrate his attention upon that rather perplexing, because mysterious, region of the spirit where political and religious feelings met in the development of medieval kingship. His first considerable work, published in 1924, was *Les Rois thaumaturges*, 'a study of the supernatural character attributed to the royal power, especially in France and England'. Its main theme was the growth of the curious practice known as 'touching for the king's evil', which most of us used to hear about in connexion with 'Good Queen Anne' and her alleged power, as a ruler of divine right, to cure scrofula. But, of course, Bloch was interested in it as the symbol and expression of an important development in religious thought and popular belief. It led him into new inquiries, for example, to the study of the cult and biographies of our last Anglo-Saxon king, Edward the Confessor. Indeed, some of us first made his acquaintance through his interest in English history, and to some scholars, interested as he had been in the study of kingship, he was always best known by the book to which I have referred. I remember vividly how one evening some twelve years later he was dining at high table in Oriel College. Another guest was a well-known German scholar, at that time spending a year in Oxford. Suddenly the German realized that the quiet reserved little man sitting on the opposite side of the table was Marc Bloch. He burst out in great excitement: 'Is that Bloch? the author of *Les Rois thaumaturges*? I have been wanting to meet him for years.' At the time I was amused by the contrast between the scene and the conventional idea of a meeting of a staid Teuton with an ebullient Gaul; now my memory of that evening arouses sadder and deeper reflections about the comradeship of scholars all over the learned world, then so promising, now broken, though we hope broken only for a time.

In the movement of international fellowship and understanding between scholars Bloch took an active part. As I have said, his book on rural France grew out of lectures given at Oslo. He was prominent in international conferences. He made his review one of the chief centres of learned studies in social history. He was in constant touch with friends and colleagues in other lands. Here in England he made many friends, especially in Cambridge and London, where he was welcomed by John Clapham and

Eileen Power and many others. English readers can judge the quality of his mind and the width of his learning in a chapter contributed by him to the first volume of the *Cambridge Economic History*. The news of his death on 16 June 1944, as it slowly and doubtfully became known to us, at first seemed unbelievable. His light had burned so brightly. This last swift little book of his, written with such passion, patriotism, and knowledge of the past, will in its English dress make him known to hundreds of people who never read his learned work—wise and clear though it is—and is his best memorial.

F. M. P.

OXFORD
January 1948

Foreword

HOW admirable it is that this 'Statement of Evidence'
could have been conceived, written, and hidden away
for our future reading at a time when France was
reeling beneath the thunder-clap of disaster.

When our world was crumbling in an appalling confusion of
men and things, when the land of Liberty, of the Rights of Man,
of spiritual grandeur and civilized elegance, had, through the
machinations of Vichy, taken on the semblance of a savage tribe
bidden to make obeisance before barbarian totems and absurd
taboos, when so many men of letters were rushing at top speed
into the open arms of slavery—how admirable, indeed, that
this great witness who, four years later, was to fall in the service
of the Resistance, could thus uncover, could thus analyse with
such lucidity, the secrets of one of the strangest defeats in all
history. Read on and you will see. . . .

I say without hesitation that, till now, no account, no explanation of, no inquiry into, the events of 1940, has appeared comparable in clarity or in firmness of design. It is right that we
should declare in no uncertain tones that this voice from the
grave of a great civilian martyr, who died without for a single
moment doubting that the dawn would break, has more true
things to tell us about the evil which plunged France into darkness, than those of any of his contemporaries.

Marc Bloch wrote this book, as he says himself, in 'a white
heat of rage'. It was the fine rage of a noble soul which would
not acquiesce, of an intelligence which refused to come to terms
with lies: it was the anger of a witness who *knew*. But this
fighter in the chaos of defeat, this historian who was compelled
to live through and endure one of the worst periods of our
history, could, nevertheless, in spite of disgust, in spite of revolt,

give to his thought and to his style a fine serenity; could view the contemporary scene with a relentlessly objective eye. *Strange Defeat* has the movement, the tone, the accent of a study which has managed to fight free of the chaotic present, of the urgent and battering tide of immediate fact. Written though it was under the pressure of experience and with a burning immediacy, with the salt of the overwhelming billows on its lips, it is as though this book had managed to create for itself an historical perspective.

That alone would suffice to make it a great book, but it contains much more than a vivid and precise description of the disaster of 1940. There is in the whole 'Statement', and particularly in the third chapter—in which a Frenchman examines his conscience—the shattering confession of a distinguished French intellectual who sets himself to examine in detail, and without mercy, a world and a caste. From that point on, the tone is that of a man meditating with fervour on others and on himself. Soldiers, politicians, civil servants, professors, workmen, peasants, all the social categories of the nation, pass beneath the microscope, and the author's conclusions are summed up with a brevity worthy of a Vauvenargues. The whole work is conceived in the lapidary terms of the 'Maxim'. Follow him in his explanation of the confusion, the terror, the ambition, and the courage of those days. Note the tranquil daring with which this man, himself the scion of the *bourgeois* aristocracy, never hesitates to find instinctively in the humble people of France the constant elements of humanity, freedom, and dignity. Marc Bloch fought in two wars, that of 1914 and that of 1939, and frequently compares them. Speaking of courage, he writes:

'... I have never come across better fighters than the miners of the Nord and the Pas de Calais whom I saw at close quarters in the first war. I found only one exception to this rule, and for a long time it puzzled me, until I discovered, quite by chance, that the man in question was a "scab", by which I mean a non-unionist employed as a strike-breaker. It is not a question of party politics. Quite simply, it comes to this, that where, in times of peace, class-loyalty is absent, the ability to put selfish interests last fails inevitably on the field of battle. . . .'

By merely reporting what he saw and heard, Captain Marc Bloch manages to paint of the High Command during the period of the 'phoney war' a series of portraits which stand out, as we know only too well, with a harsh realism. But even while he criticizes, he can focus his gaze upon the present and the future and add his comments on methods and on tactics. In all this we see the moralist and the historian guessing and foreseeing with an astonishing ease of intellectual grasp. This 'Statement of Evidence' relative to our strange defeat, written in 1940, is at once an explanation, a warning, and a confident prophecy. Now, in our newly gained liberty, it takes on a noble beauty, the kind of grandeur which belongs to all narrations of fact intended for posterity. What, for instance, he wrote in July 1940 might well serve as a golden rule for our reformers of 1946:

'. . . Whatever the complexion of its government, a country is bound to suffer if the *instruments* of power are hostile to the spirit which obtains in the various branches of its public institutions. A monarchy needs a personnel composed of monarchists. A democracy becomes hopelessly weak, and the general good suffers accordingly, if its higher officials, bred up to despise it, and necessarily drawn from those very classes the dominance of which it is pledged to destroy, serve it only half-heartedly. . . .'

Finally, the whole of Marc Bloch, all the greatness of his French humanism, is in the following lines:

'. . . How many employers of my acquaintance have I ever found capable of understanding, for instance, what nobility may lie behind a "sympathetic" strike—no matter how unreasonable? "It isn't", they say, "as though the men were striking for their *own* wages." There are two categories of Frenchmen who will never really grasp the significance of French history: those who refuse to thrill to the Consecration of our Kings at Rheims, and those who can read unmoved the account of the Festival of Federation. . . .'

The final paragraphs of Marc Bloch's 'Statement' open with this sort of *largo* movement:

'. . . The generation to which I belong has a bad conscience. . . .'

I defy any Frenchman who is sensitive to the motions of the spirit to read this passage without feeling something of that emotion which moves us in the presence of perfect human dignity. One finds the same purity in the simple phrases in which Marc Bloch of the Resistance expressed his last wishes to his family in the event of his sudden death. As early as 1940 he had foreseen that he would have to take up arms again and embark on a new struggle, and a fresh adventure—the adventure of Civilian Resistance in the heart of occupied France:

'. . . My only hope, and I make no bones about it, is that when the moment comes we shall have enough blood left to shed, even though it be the blood of those who are dear to us (I say nothing of my own, to which I attach no importance). For there can be no salvation where there is not some sacrifice, and no national liberty in the fullest sense unless we have ourselves worked to bring it about. . . .'

Marc Bloch was right, and right, too, in his summing up:

'. . . Whatever form the final triumph may take, it will be many years before the stain of 1940 can be effaced.'

This 'Statement' of his is a light shining through the darkness.

The intellectual leaders of the nation, the university world, those in France who care for the things of the mind and the imagination, all know, only too well, what they have lost in him.

Each of Marc Bloch's books, *Les Rois thaumaturges, Les Caractères originaux de l'histoire rurale française, La Société féodale,* represented a discovery, stood for yet one more triumph of modern historical science over the past. His colleagues, his students, workers everywhere in the field of history, a vast public of chosen spirits in all the countries of the world, knew

Marc Bloch as a thinker of infinite curiosity, as one of those writers who, more than others, had brought something new to historical research. France could be proud of him. 'I remember', says the British Professor Brogan, 'I remember vividly the day on which the news of Marc Bloch's death reached us in Cambridge, and how eagerly we pounced on the rumour—false, alas!—that he had escaped. When we learned beyond doubt that he was dead, we felt that a blow had been dealt to the whole world of learning.' There can be no doubt that he was a great figure, or that his work will endure. Generations still to come of students, researchers, and scholars will find in it a rich harvest.

When he joined the Resistance with us at Lyons I already knew him by reputation. What I did not know was that a man might, as he did, impart to his very life the same style as marked the movement of his spirit and intelligence.

. . . Dear Marc Bloch, dear 'Narbonne' in the Resistance. . . . At the beginning of this 'Statement' of his, speaking of the fact that he was a Jew, a fact about which he felt 'neither pride nor shame', he says:

'. . . that France, from which many would like to expel me to-day (and may, for all I know, succeed in doing so), will remain, whatever happens, the one country with which my deepest emotions are inextricably bound up. I was born in France. I have drunk of the waters of her culture. I have made her past my own. I breathe freely only in her climate, and I have done my best, with others, to defend her interests. . . .'

'They' never succeeded in expelling him from his native soil, from the spirit of France, or from the struggle she was waging. The most 'they' could do was to expel him from life. . . . He offered his blood even before it was asked of him. And yet . . .

For a long time we would not believe that the brutes had extinguished that light.

It was bad enough to know that he had been beaten, tortured;

that the body of this slim man on which distinction sat with so natural an air, that this refined, moderate-minded, proud intellectual had been plunged into an ice-cold bath, and then, choking and shivering, had been struck, beaten, and outraged.

We could not, literally could not, bear to contemplate the picture which this news conjured up: could not bear to think of Marc Bloch, that perfect type of French dignity, that fine example of a deep and exquisite humanism, in the hands of the Nazi beasts: could not endure the knowledge of that lovely spirit degraded to a mere thing of flesh in the vilest of vile hands. . . . A few of us, his friends, his comrades in the secret battle, happened to be together at Lyons when we heard of his arrest. Somebody, all of a sudden, said: 'They have tortured him.' A fellow prisoner had seen him at Gestapo headquarters, bleeding from the mouth (a blood-stained gash in place of that mischievous smile which had been his last gift to me as we stood together at a street corner just before the horror had pounced!). I remember how, at those words, 'he was bleeding', tears of rage leapt to the eyes of all of us. Even the toughest bowed their heads, overwhelmed by the news, as men may do when injustice has exceeded all bounds.

For months we had been waiting, hoping. Deported?—no—still in the prison of Montluc at Lyons?—transferred to another city? We knew nothing until the day came when we were told, 'No hope now: he was shot at Trévoux on the 16th June, 1944. His clothes, his papers, were identified.' They killed him along with a few others who had found strength in his courage.

For it is known in what manner he died. A boy of sixteen was standing next to him, trembling. 'Will it hurt?' Marc Bloch took him affectionately by the arm, and merely said, 'No, my boy: it won't hurt at all.' He was the first to fall, crying 'Vive La France!'

There is something in the phrasing of those last words that is at once familiar and sublime, something that belongs to the

simplicity of the great and antique world. To me it speaks of the
serene integrity of a life which, from its deep, new delving into
the past, unearthed the eternal values of the human spirit—of an
active faith for which he knew how to die.

I can see again in memory that charming moment when
twenty-year-old Maurice, the youngest of our underground
'group', blushed with pleasure as he presented his 'new recruit',
a gentleman of fifty, with a rosette in his buttonhole, a thin,
refined face, silver-grey hair, and keen eyes behind a pair of
spectacles. He was carrying a brief-case in one hand, a walking-
stick in the other. At first his manners were a little stiff, but,
after the first few seconds, he smiled, held out his hand, and said
politely: 'Yes, I'm Maurice's "colt". . . .' It was thus, with a
smile, that Professor Marc Bloch joined the Resistance. With
a smile no different he was to leave it for the last time.

Very early on in our breathless, hunted, necessarily Bohemian
existence, I was filled with admiration for the intense love of
order and method which was our 'dear Master's' gift to us.
(That rather academic phrase seemed no less comic to him than
it did to us. It was, so to speak, the relic of a past which, however
real it had once been, seemed now so very far away from, so
unconnected with, our daily preoccupations—rather as a top hat
might have looked on a man armed with a tommy-gun.) The
same 'dear Master' now turned with eagerness to absorb the
rudiments of outlawry and rebellion. We soon grew accustomed
to the spectacle of this Sorbonne professor sharing with us, out-
wardly unmoved, that life of the 'pariah dog' which was what
the underground movement in our cities meant.

I know that I am not running counter to his deepest feelings
when I say that he loved danger, that he had, in Bossuet's words,
'the soul of the fighter that rules the body of its possessor'. He
had refused to accept the Armistice and Pétain. In the post where
Destiny had placed him he carried on the battle. But in the

hustle and bustle of our secret work he brought to our every meeting, our every council-of-war, to our duties, our rashness and our risks, a taste for precision, for detail, for logic which lay like a somewhat ridiculous piece of decoration on the surface of his calm courage, and which I, for my part, found enchanting.

'Come, come, we mustn't let ourselves be carried away. The great thing is to isolate and *limit* the problem. . . .'—whether that problem was getting instructions through to the local leaders of the M.U.R. (*Mouvements Unis de Résistance*), to arrange for the transport of arms, to print some clandestine leaflet, or to make sure that the authorities of the 'Underground' knew precisely what to do on D-day. . . .

When, at some street corner, I saw Marc Bloch, his coat collar turned up against the cold, his walking-stick in his hand, 'passing' mysterious and compromising scraps of paper to young men in trappers' coats or pullovers, as calmly as though he were handing back their essays to a lot of competitors in an examination, I used to tell myself—as I still do—that nobody who had not lived through those days could have the slightest idea what exaltation was to be found in the secret civilian Resistance of France.

The Gestapo, the Militia, the Pétain Police, were beside themselves with fury. Each day one of our friends, as we said, 'got it'. He would be there with us, and then, a moment later, gone, spirited away, swallowed up, as it were, in the abyss. There were always others to take his place. But how long the time seemed! Hope grew sick and weary. Victory and the end of the nightmare were so far off! But still the *maquis* fought, still the secret presses printed, and the deep, relentless voice of the Resistance could be heard behind and above everything. There were searches, arrests, bursts of firing in the streets, tortures, shootings. . . . How lonely we felt sometimes seeing all around us apathy, acquiescence—and hideous examples of collaboration.

Very soon Marc Bloch was known to the whole Resistance movement—known far too well. He saw, insisted on seeing, too many people. He had carried over from the days of his law-abiding life as a university professor the conviction that no one else can do one's work for one. He wanted to do as much as he possibly could himself. He had a passion for organization. He was quite rightly obsessed by the need to see that every wheel was turning smoothly in the whole. vast and complicated machine by means of which the M.U.R. issued instructions to the *maquis*, the *francs-tireurs*, the propaganda services, the Press, and arranged for acts of sabotage, for attacks on the Occupying Power, for the struggle against the deportation of workers. His was a fighter's, not a soldier's temperament—not a soldier's, I mean, in the professional sense. 'In the '14 war', he used to say jokingly, 'I never managed to get promotion. D'you realize that I am the *oldest* Captain in the whole of the French Army?'

He had, like all of us, to conceal his identity beneath a double, a triple, a quadruple alibi: one for his false papers, one for use among his colleagues, one for signing letters. What induced him, in the early days, to use the odd pseudonym of 'Arpajon'? I think it amused him to conjure up the thought of that small suburban town, and the picturesque steam train which in those days puffed its way nightly from the Central Markets through the Quartier Latin—*his* Quartier, with its schools and colleges. When 'they'—as we said—'got wise' to the name, he decided to remain loyal to the same railway system, and changed to 'Chevreuse'. But they 'got wise' to Chevreuse too, and we thought it wiser for him to get out of the Île de France for good and all. So he became 'Narbonne'. . . . It was as Narbonne that he served as delegate of the *franc-tireur* group to the regional committee of the M.U.R. at Lyons. It was as Narbonne that, in company with the Delegates of 'Combat' and 'Liberation', he was to direct the whole of the Lyons Resistance until that tragic day when the trap closed and he was dragged away to execution.

'Narbonne' he was for the Resistance, but for the landlords of the houses where he lodged, Monsieur Blanchard. It was under that name that he did his travelling, made journeys, for instance, to Paris, for the meetings of the C.G.E. (*Comité Générale d'Études de la Résistance*). There was an element of 'sport' about the zest with which he accepted the risks and outlawry of his new life. There was a youthfulness, an air of physical fitness, about him at which I never ceased to wonder when I used to see him run to catch the tram which took him back to his Lyons lodgings up behind the Croix-Rousse—a chance find, the principal feature of which was a kitchen-range which came in very useful when, at regular intervals, he set about burning his excessive accumulation of papers.

I often used to fetch him from the quiet, countrified rue de l'Orangerie at Cuire. It was arranged between us that I should never go upstairs, but should stand in the street and whistle a few bars of Beethoven or Wagner to bring him down—usually the first bars of the *Ride of the Valkyries*. He would run downstairs with a grin on his face, and never failed to say: 'Not bad, Chabot: but never quite in tune, you know. . . .'

Imagine this man, made for the silence of creative work, for the studious calm of a book-filled library, hurrying from street to street, helping us to decipher the Resistance dispatches in the attic of some old Lyons house. . . .

And then came catastrophe. After trying for a whole year, the Gestapo managed at last to lay hands on part of the M.U.R. headquarters staff. Marc Bloch was arrested, tortured, imprisoned. I have already described the wonderful way in which he met his end. . . .

On 26 June 1944 twenty-seven corpses were dug up at Saint-Didier-sur-Formont, near Lyons. Some friends managed to get hold of the police photographs. We studied them anxiously. The face of an old man with a ten days' growth of white beard, a scrap of clothing marked with the initials M.B., a set of false papers in the name of Maurice Blanchard. . . . Yes, it was Marc Bloch right enough.

'If I get out of this alive, I shall go back to my teaching'—he frequently used to say.

He was passionately devoted to his chosen work. He dreamed of wide-spreading educational reforms of which he published the general lines in the clandestine review called *Les Cahiers politiques*. He adored his family: his brave, sweet wife who died suddenly while he was confined at Montluc, and his six children —Alice, Étienne, Louis, Daniel, Jean-Paul, Suzanne. . . .

I have rarely known any man whose intelligence and heart and bearing were marked by so natural an air of distinction. Spontaneously he measured all things by the standards of human values and spiritual truth. What he felt in those days of constant alarms and activity, of being pursued and having to get away at a moment's notice, of outlawry and conspiracy, was the need not, as the phrase is, to 'escape', but to return to the true mental atmosphere of the life he loved, the life of thought and art.

I remember one night of full moon on the Croix-Rousse. I was walking back with Marc Bloch to his remote hide-out. So unoppressive did the darkness seem, so far removed from the stifling drama of our lives, that the fancy took him to talk of music and of poetry—not in order to forget the risks and the horror, but so that he might evoke something of the fine discipline of the mind, of the gentle beauties now profaned, banished, and temporarily eclipsed, which alone justify the life of human beings, and for which he, Marc Bloch, was fighting.

He always had a book in his hand when he was out on duty. He used it not only for reading but for jotting down the details of secret meetings in a mysterious system of cryptograms which was his peculiar pride. But he was careful to choose his authors carefully so as not to waste his time.

The last I saw him carrying were a Ronsard . . . and a collection of French medieval folk-songs.

GEORGES ALTMAN
(Chabot)

Translator's Note

For the information contained in the notes on pages 139 and 143 I am indebted to Monsieur René Varin, C.B.E., of the French Embassy in London, and wish to express my gratitude for his help.

xx

STRANGE DEFEAT

Chapter One

PRESENTATION OF THE WITNESS

WILL these pages ever be published?—I cannot tell. But whatever the eventual answer to that question may be, it seems probable that, for a long time to come, those outside the circle of my immediate intimates will be able to read them only 'under the rose'. Nevertheless, I have quite made up my mind to proceed with the writing of them, though the effort involved will be harsh and exacting. How much easier it would be to plead weariness and discouragement as an excuse for doing nothing! But if the kind of documentation that I plan is to have any value, it must be put into shape at once while the subject is still fresh and living in my memory. Nor can I really persuade myself that the effort will be wholly useless. A day will come, of that I am convinced, after no matter how long a delay, when this old and sacred soil of France, from which, in the past, so many harvests have been lifted—harvests of free thought and of judgement unrestrained—will once more burgeon into ripeness. In that happier future many secret records will be made public. Gradually the mists of ignorance and malice, which now begin to gather about the most terrible collapse in all the long story of our national life, will thin. It may be that then, those on whom the duty falls of seeing through them to the truth beyond will be helped in their task by glancing at the pages (should they come their way) in which an eyewitness has set down the events of the year 1940, just as he experienced them.

It is no part of my intention to produce a book of reminiscences. The account of what happened to one soldier among many is of no especial interest now when we are concerned with matters of greater moment than the details of personal adventure,

1

however picturesque, however amusing, these may have been. But it is always well to have a full description of the witness in the box, and I feel that before narrating the things I saw I should give some account of the man who saw them.

For something like thirty-four years I have been wholly occupied with the writing and the teaching of history. In the course of my professional career I have had to examine a great many documents belonging to a great many periods of the past, and, as best I might, sift what is true in them from what is false. I have had, too, to keep a watchful eye on the world around me, holding it to be the historian's prime duty—in the words of my master, Pirenne—'to show a keen interest in life'. The special study which, in the course of my researches, I have made of the life of the country-side has convinced me that we can truly understand the past only if we read it by the light of the present. For a sound historian of rural economy a keen eye for the shapes of fields is no less necessary than an aptitude for deciphering the crabbed records of an earlier day. I have done my best to bring to the tragic events in which I played a modest part the same habits of criticism, of observation, and, I trust, of integrity, which were bred in me by the exigencies of my work as an historian.

My chosen calling is generally considered to be peculiarly lacking in adventure. But Destiny decided that I, with most of my generation, should, on two separate occasions, separated from one another by a stretch of twenty-one years, be jerked violently from the ways of peace. Whatever other results this breach of the normal routine of teaching may have had, it certainly made it possible for me to enjoy an unusually wide experience of the many different aspects of a nation in arms. I have served in two wars. I began the first, in August 1914, as an infantry sergeant: in other words, as an ordinary 'foot-slogger', only just above the level of a private. In the course of the next four years I became successively a Platoon Commander, an Intelligence Officer, an A.D.C. at Regimental Headquarters, and finished up as a Captain on a Corps Staff. My second experience as a soldier was, for the most part, gained at the very opposite end of the hierarchic scale. My duties confined me to the immediate entourage of an army commander, and involved me in constant liaison with G.H.Q. The fall of the cards has brought me plenty of variety, and has introduced me to a cross-section not only of the Army but of humanity in general.

By birth I am a Jew, though not by religion, for I have never professed any creed, whether Hebrew or Christian. I feel neither pride nor shame in my origins. I am, I hope, a sufficiently good historian to know that racial qualities are a myth, and that the whole notion of Race is an absurdity which becomes particularly flagrant when attempts are made to apply it, as in this particular case of the Jews, to a group of co-religionists originally brought together from every corner of the Mediterranean, Turco-Khazar, and Slav worlds. I am at pains never to stress my heredity save when I find myself in the presence of an anti-Semite. But it may be that certain persons will challenge the evidence which I propose to put on record, and attempt to discredit it on the grounds that I am an 'alien'. I need say no more in rebuttal of such a charge than that my great-grandfather was a serving soldier in 1793; that my father was one of the defenders of Strasbourg in 1870; that both my uncles chose to leave their native Alsace after its annexation by the Second Reich; that I was brought up in the traditions of patriotism which found no more fervent champions than the Jews of the Alsatian exodus, and that France, from which many would like to expel me to-day (and may, for all I know, succeed in doing so), will remain, whatever happens, the one country with which my deepest emotions are inextricably bound up. I was born in France. I have drunk of the waters of her culture. I have made her past my own. I breathe freely only in her climate, and I have done my best, with others, to defend her interests.

One day when I stood chatting with a young officer in a

3

doorway at Malo-les-Bains, during a bombing raid, he said to me: 'This war has taught me a lot, and one of its greatest lessons has been that there are a great many professional soldiers who will never be fighters, and a whole heap of civilians who have fighting in their blood. That', he went on, 'is a truth I should never have suspected before the 10th of May. You, for instance, are a born fighter.' The judgement may appear to be rather over-simple, but I believe it to contain a good deal of truth, both as a generalization, and (to be perfectly sincere) when applied to my own particular case. An army doctor whom I knew when I was on the staff as an intelligence officer loved to twit me in a kindly way about being an 'old professor' who had 'more of the soldier in him than all the rest of the bunch put together'—which meant merely, I imagine, that I had a weakness for orderliness in the handling of military matters. I emerged from the first war with four decorations, and I do not think I flatter myself unduly when I say that but for the sudden irruption of the Germans into Rennes, which put a sudden stop to all recommendations from the First Army, I could hardly have avoided going home after this one, too, with another ribbon on my tunic.[1] In 1915, after convalescing in hospital, I returned to the front before I need have done, as a volunteer. In 1939 I allowed my name to be kept on the active list in spite of the fact that my age and my six children gave me a perfect right to put my uniform away in mothballs. I mention these things not from any motive of vainglory. I have known far too many brave and humble men who did their duty without fuss or bother (far better than I could ever claim to have done mine), to be guilty of the sin of boasting. I put them on record here simply and solely as a form of self-protection against criticism. At times I may be rather crudely outspoken, and the reader may be tempted to accuse me of prejudice. To him I would say that I have always been an enemy to soft-soap, that I served of my own free will as a soldier, and that

[1] The award was actually made in Corps Orders dated July 1942.

in the opinion of seniors and comrades alike I did a reasonably good job.

That is a bald statement of what I was expected to do, and, consequently, of what I was in a position to see, in the course of the last war.

In the period between the two wars I more than once refused, as I have already said, to take advantage of a regulation which would have enabled me to escape from further military service. But though from 1919 onwards I figured as a Reserve Officer eligible for staff duties, I made no attempt to attend any of the so-called 'refresher' courses. This, generally speaking, I admit was wrong. The only excuse I can plead is that the years in question happened to coincide with the period of my life during which, for good or for ill, I was producing the bulk of my serious historical work, and that therefore I had very little leisure. I derive, however, a certain amount of consolation for my failure from my active experiences during the campaign. I feel quite sure that the kind of training given at the Staff College which I was thus spared would have done nothing to fit me for my duties. But since, at that time, the military authorities attached particular importance to graduating with distinction from that establishment, I was made to suffer for having played truant. I received, in fact, a double punishment. In 1918 I had attained the rank of captain, and it was as a captain, therefore, that I was called up first in 1938, and again in August 1939, in spite of being recommended for promotion by senior officers who had had occasion to see something of my work. A captain I remained until I was demobilized on 11 July 1940. That was the first consequence of my slackness. It left me without any feeling of resentment or even of sorrow. The second related to the nature of the duties I was called upon to perform.

I had originally been attached, on paper, to Intelligence at Corps level. It seemed a reasonable form of employment for a professional historian. I was, however, almost immediately degraded to a similar position with a division. Soon afterwards I was withdrawn altogether from duty with an active formation, and relegated to the rather inglorious job of area administration, being attached to a headquarters controlling a group of sub-divisional areas. Since, however, this particular group was based on Strasbourg, which was generally expected to be one of the first targets for German bombing, I felt some qualms about agitating for a transfer. A natural laziness combined with this feeling to prevent me from taking any steps to find more interesting employment. One of my friends had tried, even before the war, to get me attached to G.H.Q. Intelligence, but there had not been sufficient time for his representations to produce results. Consequently, after two short periods of preliminary training, I was appointed to the Strasbourg Group of subdivisional areas, first in September 1938 at the time of the Munich crisis, again, for a few hours only, when in March 1939 I was hastily summoned from Cambridge, and finally on 24 August in that same year of destiny.

By and large I have never really regretted this appointment. The duties devolving upon a subdivisional Group Headquarters are, in themselves, flat and dismal enough, but they do, in the early stages of hostilities, afford one a good vantage-point from which to observe the general scene. That, at least, was my experience during the first two or three weeks.

We had to supervise a good deal of the actual mobilization. What happened in similar commands situated farther back? I imagine that, after the first excitement was over, they managed to keep pretty busy with paper-work and details. My own, which soon moved from Strasbourg to Molsheim in the foothills of the Vosges, was very much in the thick of things. When, at long last and extraordinarily slowly, the Sixth Army got its own organization going, our rôle, which had already been progressively whittled down, was reduced almost to zero. There followed an interminable succession of days when, seemingly, nothing ever got done. Our little party consisted of five persons: a general of brigade, a lieutenant-colonel, two captains, and a lieutenant. We used to spend the time sitting in the schoolroom which formed our office (I can still see the scene vividly in memory), longing for a runner to arrive unexpectedly with some official form which would provide us with an excuse for filling up still further forms. The most contented of the lot was the younger of the two captains, whose duty it was to issue passes! An historian is not often bored. He always has the resources of memory, observation, and writing to keep him busy. But the feeling that one is serving no useful purpose in a nation at war is intolerable.

Our general was a reservist, a thoroughly good fellow who was eventually sent home to pursue his studies. These, for the most part, took the form of fly-fishing. What remained of his staff was merged with the subdivisional area group based on Saverne. I spent only two days in that agreeable though definitely overcrowded little town. I had managed to make contact with a high-ranking officer at G.H.Q. Wire-pulling with the object of landing a better job is not an activity in which one naturally takes much pride, but it was scarcely my fault that only thus could I find any useful outlet for my enthusiasm. Thanks to my influential friend, I was transferred early in October to H.Q., First Army, and reported, without losing a moment, at Bohain in Picardy.

G.H.Q. had made it quite clear what my function was to be. I was to act as liaison officer with the British, and, as such, was attached to the Intelligence Branch. But I had been there only a short time when two other officers turned up with precisely similar instructions. The Chief of Staff, embarrassed by a super-fluity of riches, decided that each main formation of the Army should have its own organ of contact with the Expeditionary Force. He therefore divided us up among the various administra-tive branches—omitting only 'A', which, being concerned with

7

matters of personnel and discipline, has no need of links with the outside world. I found myself attached to 'Q'—that is to say, to the office in charge of transport, labour-supply, and rations, though my job was very much what it had previously been, a combination of Intelligence and Diplomacy. I shall explain later on how, most unfortunately, and certainly against my will, it lost, in fact, any significance it may once have had.

I began to wonder whether I was fated to drop back into that lazy existence of which I had once already been a victim. I was feeling thoroughly lost and dispirited when it happened that the officer in charge of petrol-supplies was moved elsewhere and I inherited his duties.

Almost overnight I had become the mighty Fuel King of the most heavily motorized army on the whole of the French front. My first reaction was one of sheer panic. I realized only too well that, in the event of active operations, I should have to shoulder the most appalling responsibilities. I did not know the first thing about the subject. 'Pray God', I wrote to my wife, 'that Hitler decides to go slow for a week or two!' There are, however, few administrative posts that the ordinary intelligent man cannot tackle reasonably well, provided he gives his mind to the job. I did my very best to learn everything I could about what would be expected of me, and was blessed at the outset by a piece of real good luck. I found at the Army lorry park the wisest and most un-self-regarding counsellor that any man in my position could have wished for. This is the first time I have had occasion to mention the name of Captain Lachamp: it will certainly not be the last. The bitter aftertaste left in my mouth by the memory of this bungled and tragic war makes me the more inclined to cherish the few bright spots which it could show. It is always a delight to meet a man who really is a man. There can be no greater reward than to work with such a colleague in perfect harmony, and to feel the day-to-day sharing of one's problems blossoming into a genuine and solid friendship.

Truth to tell, my new functions, once I had learned my way about, demanded little in the way of hard work. The period of apprenticeship once over, I slipped back, like everybody else, into the unexciting existence of the military bureaucrat. Not that I was ever left to kick my heels, but I was certainly never hag-ridden by my work, and the amount of stimulus that I received from the daily routine was small. Fortunately, I was able, for some weeks, to combine with it an additional task which I undertook quite voluntarily. It came to my notice that the information at our disposition about petrol dumps situated on Belgian territory was absurdly insufficient. This lack of accurate knowledge was particularly serious in view of the well-known fact that, once the Germans had violated the frontier, we should be called upon to move into Belgium. Certain personal contacts made it possible for me to add considerably to the headquarters file on this subject. A good deal of rather ticklish negotiating had to be done, and here my experience of the ways and mentality of staff officers served me in good stead. In particular I learned the very special way in which the bureaucrat who has a reasonable dose of good manners can interpret the phrase 'meddling in what doesn't concern one'. By and large, the inquiry which I set on foot, valuable though it may have turned out to be, did not really fall within my competence. My conduct in the matter was what is sometimes called (with a discreet smile) 'dynamic'.

This occupation, however, lasted only a short while, and once the goal at which I aimed had been reached, I was reduced to a daily grind which consisted in counting petrol-tins and rationing every drop of fuel issued. It was natural, therefore, though perhaps foolish, that I should once again sink into a mood of despondency and feel that what intellectual powers and gifts of initiative I might have were not being employed to the best advantage. The tedium of those long winter and spring months of 1939–40 wore down the resistance of a great many intelligent men. I was, I suppose, like many others, the victim of a peculiarly

9

subtle form of poisoning. Be that as it may, I quite seriously thought of asking, once the summer was over, for permission to resume my labours at the Sorbonne. But before I could take any step in the matter, the storm of 10 May burst over our heads.

How unexpected it was can best be shown by mentioning something quite trivial that happened to me personally. I had gone to Paris on the 9th, with the object of proceeding to Meaux early the next morning, in order to get from G.H.Q. Transport a supply of the petrol-coupons by means of which I kept a check on the fuel consumption of my various units. I arrived at Meaux in complete ignorance of what had happened the previous night. The gentlemen at G.H.Q. showed no little surprise at the sudden apparition of an officer who had made a special journey, for so very unwarlike a purpose, from one of the armies on the Belgian frontier! After a few moments spent in talking at cross-purposes, I realized why it was that I had been so coldly received. I had just time to make the station, cross Paris, fight my way on to an incredibly overcrowded train, and so get back to my battle-post.

I have promised myself not to describe in detail the three weeks that followed. I shall have occasion, later, to set down the lessons of what then occurred. A few scenes, chosen from among the crowd that presses on my memory, will suffice to mark the progress of a series of days and nights crammed with the incidents of that tragic campaign of the Nord.

Let me begin by making mention of the girls' school at Valenciennes which we planned to occupy temporarily before moving on to an Advanced H.Q. in Belgium which had been chosen on the assumption that we should be engaged in open warfare, though, in fact, it was never used. It was our first experience at close range of the ruin caused by the German preliminary bombing attack.

On two occasions I was able to slip away on trips into Belgium. They suited that nomadic instinct in me of which my superiors did not always approve. On the 11th I got no farther than Mons, but on the 12th I pushed forward in the direction of Nivelles, Fleurus, and Charleroi. All along the road we saw miners enjoying the temporary leisure of the Easter holiday. They were standing at the doors of their houses to give a welcome to the French motorized columns. The gently rolling country-side round Ligny and Quatre-Bras, where once Ney's army had fought, decked in the green of early spring, presented a charming scene. But already the sides of the thoroughfare were chock-a-block with long lines of civilians making their way back from the districts round Liège. They trudged along, pushing the now almost traditional children's prams piled high with every variety of ill-assorted baggage. A sprinkling of disbanded Belgian soldiers from the villages through which they had passed was symptomatic of a more alarming state of affairs. Anxiety began to press hard on the heels of an earlier optimism. Word went round that the passages of the Meuse had been forced. An effort had been made to get supplies up to the divisions which had been hastily rushed into action, almost immediately to lose all cohesion and vanish, so it seemed, into thin air. Ultimately, our Army withdrew towards the south-west and, on the 18th, H.Q. was moved back to Douai.

For rather less than two days we occupied yet another school in the suburbs of that town. Having already enjoyed the hospitality of a girls' school at Bohain, we felt that educational establishments were to be our fate. All around us bombs were showering down on the station, the main roads, and the aerodromes. Almost every day news came in that yet another 'back-area' fuel dump had fallen into German hands. The fine containers which we had constructed at Saint-Quentin and Cambrai, and were holding jealously in reserve in order to ensure a continuous flow of petrol to the front, the 'dispersed' depots of which we had been so proud, where the tins were cleverly camouflaged under the trees of public parks or in the lean-tos of abandoned brickfields, could no longer be relied upon to supply the needs of our formations. After the shortest of delays we had to pack up once again and resume our trek. It had been at first arranged that I should be left behind with two assistants at Advanced H.Q., Douai. But that plan, like so many others, had to be revised a few hours later. Picking my way across the blackened country-side, through a maze of slag-heaps, most of which had collapsed grotesquely under the effect of bombing, and had already lost their pristine clarity of outline, I reached the fourth—and last—school, at Lens, which we were destined to occupy (19 May).

This time it was a nursery school. The furniture had been designed to fit the requirements of very young children, with the result that we were faced with a choice between two kinds of physical distress. Either we could remain standing indefinitely— an exhausting process—or we could squat on seats that were far too narrow for our mature figures, and at the imminent risk of skinning our knees against the undersides of the desks. Not that one was always in a position to choose. One might be forced into a sitting posture by the necessity of scribbling an urgent message, but then, how in the world was one to get up again? To extricate oneself from the seat of tribulation demanded strenuous and prolonged effort. This curious form of ordeal, the ugliness of the landscape, the filthy coal-dust that filtered incessantly through every crack and cranny—everything about the gloomy spot seemed to make a fitting background to our growing mood of depression. As a Battle H.Q., this educational set-up at Lens was sheer hell, a fitting preliminary to defeat. Shall I ever, I wonder, forget that evening of 20 May? Just as it was getting dusk, with the flames of Arras lighting the distant horizon, my immediate superior came into the room. In a very low voice, and pointing on a school wall-map to the mouth of the Somme, he said: 'The Boches are *there*!'—then, turning away, he murmured, 'Don't talk about it more than you can help.' I had been trying to get G.H.Q. on the telephone, and it was only after I had made the attempt several times and failed, that I realized to the full the sense of complete abandonment that comes to a soldier when he hears the word—'surrounded'.

A little later (22 May) we migrated northwards, and fetched up at Estaires-sur-Lys. But this, being a traffic-centre, was not a very healthy spot. German pilots did not often make a dead set at buildings occupied by H.Q. staffs, but it was too much to expect that we should not occasionally be hit. On the very first afternoon of our being there, a bomb fell near enough to shake the walls and chimney of the inn where we had established our office. The burst was sufficiently close to cover our clothes, papers, and faces with an indescribably filthy contribution of soot. The warning was not ignored. I had just turned in, and was enjoying the luxury of sheets for the first time for many days (for the last, too, it turned out, during the campaign) when a movement-order dragged me from my bed in the middle of the night. As a matter of fact we did not get off until well after dawn. The authorities always showed a curious inability to organize that most necessary of all things—rest. In the course of the following morning, after making a long detour which, as usual, involved a severe dislocation of my fuel supplies, I reached the Château of Attiches, south of Lille, whither I had been pre-ceded by the rest of the staff (23 May).

The château stood in a fine stretch of park-land. It was a graceless building adorned on the outside with a repellent arrange-ment of 'artistic' tiles, and filled with the kind of luxurious, gloomy, and vaguely medieval furniture which the rich middle-class families of the later nineteenth century regarded as the necessary background to a bogus territorial grandeur. In one corner of the dining-room, where we worked, the owner, with what we could not but consider rather premature consideration, had erected a pile of mortuary wreaths. It was here, on the after-noon of the 23rd, that our 'Q' branch finally split into two sections. One of these was to form our rear organization, and at once proceeded to the coast, there to arrange a system of sea-borne communications. The other—to which I was attached—stayed where it was with the army commander. As things turned out, the former, though at a much greater distance from the front, was to come in for the worst of the bombing—an irony of fate which nobody at the time had, I suspect, foreseen. In the innocence of our hearts, we of the forward elements fully expected to be the chosen target for air-attack (bombs did, indeed, fall continuously all round us) and were quite prepared to find ourselves exposed to the imminent danger of capture. Since, too, rear H.Q. contained, in addition to several men whose courage was beyond question, a fair sprinkling of those who were not averse to putting a few miles between themselves and the battle-front, we of the front line had a feeling that we formed a rather special body of the elect, imbued with the spirit of comradeship and mutual assistance. So strong was this prejudice that one of my companions, a plain lieutenant of reserve who, in civil life, was President of a Chamber of Commerce in the Nord Department, having been told to report for duty to the coast, obstinately refused to budge. The second-in-command of our section, who, in a way not calculated to improve morale, had ignored the generally accepted military tradition in these matters, and moved back with his immediate superior, took in very ill part an attitude so clearly at variance with his own. White with anger, he haled the disobedient underling before the highest disciplinary authority available, only to find, to his great surprise, that this courageous refusal to obey orders was by no means frowned upon.

Another scene is associated in my memory with that dining-room at Attiches. It had to do with one of the most degrading spectacles of human weakness that it has ever been my lot to witness. As the morning wore on we became aware of the figure of a man slumped in a chair close to the door. Dull-eyed and gloomy, he sat there chewing innumerable cigarettes. He wore no badges of rank on his sleeve, and the personnel of the office pushed past him with no more consideration than they would have accorded to the lowest orderly. He was, in fact, a general of division who had been deprived of his command a few hours previously—for drunkenness, it was said, though with what justice I do not know. He was waiting to have a final interview with the army commander. This he obtained, after considerable delay, about noon. It lasted only a few minutes, and that was the last we saw of our depressing visitor.

On the 26th we moved into what was to be our last head-quarters, a gay little villa, furnished with refinement, situated at Steenwerck, to the north-west of Lille. The house next door was occupied by General Prioux. He had just taken over command of the Army from General Blanchard. The latter had been trans-ferred to the Army Group, thereby escaping the immediate consequences of the disaster. Enemy pressure was becoming more and more accentuated, and we were faced by the imminent necessity of burning our important reserve fuel dumps at Lille. I spent the whole of the 27th and the night following in an attempt to get a decision on this point. No less than four separate orders were issued, and no less than four times were they countermanded. The last of them was within an ace of never being carried out. I dispatched a messenger on a motor-bike after dark, but he never arrived. What happened to him I do not know. My conscience, however, was clear. I had to see that the order reached its destination. Had I taken it myself I should have been guilty of dereliction of duty. Still, it was only natural that I should feel some slight pang at the thought that, quite possibly, I had sent a brave man to his death. A number of similar incidents remained in my memory from the last war. For a while they had had a way of haunting me when I could not sleep, though eventually I became callous. Fortunately, on this occasion I was able to get a second message through, and the dump went up just in time. But only just in time, for the Army had already begun a withdrawal behind the line of the Lys, preparatory to a general movement seawards. Not the whole of the Army, however, was involved. On the evening of the 28th, General Prioux made it known to us that he despaired of being able to disengage two, and possibly more, of his divisions. Consequently, he had decided to remain in person at Steenwerck, there to await the coming of the enemy. It was his intention to keep with him only one or two officers. The rest of us, he said, had better make for the coast under cover of darkness, and get on board what ships we could find. A little later I went to see him in order to get a confirmation of the order that I was to empty, render useless, and abandon my mobile tanks. This meant depriving the Army of its last few remaining gallons of petrol, and I felt that I could not take it upon myself to make so grave a decision, though it was a logical result of the situation as it was at that time developing. Our great-hearted leader was sadly pacing the hall of the house in which he had his quarters. His had been a melancholy fate if ever there was one. Seconded from the Cavalry Corps which, so I am told, he had commanded with distinction, he was sent at the eleventh hour to take over an army already in a state of disintegration, and had to accept a captivity which he had ill deserved in place of the man who was really responsible for the defeat.

That duty done, I returned to our villa. In the course of the day I had already, acting on instructions, burned all our records, including the note-book in which I had kept a day-to-day diary of my own adventures. I would give a great deal to have that green-bound volume by me now. I also committed all my personal correspondence to the mess stove—for we had been forbidden to load ourselves with unnecessary baggage—and made what room I could in my haversack for a few especially precious or useful objects. As it was, I forgot about three-quarters of them, though I was at least able to change my working tunic for something in a rather better state of repair. In this I

16

was more fortunate than the general commanding the Army artillery. This fine soldier who, from a perhaps excessive scruple of honour, had decided to remain with General Prioux, was separated from all his belongings, which had been sent, rather prematurely, to Dunkirk. He had only the clothes he stood up in, and there was a hole in the elbow of his tunic. This misfortune made him voluble. He could face the prospect of captivity calmly enough—but not of captivity in rags!

We left that night: a long, slow column of cars moving across the Belgian country-side, for the French roads were already cut. By first light we had covered barely ten kilometres. How had we managed to evade the enemy's motorized scouts? To this day I do not really know. The fact remains that, sometimes on foot, sometimes on wheels, I reached Hondschoote round about noon. But I still had to make the coast. Together with Captain Lachamp, whom I found there on my arrival, I set about discovering the main fuel column which had started ahead of us with instructions to rendezvous at Bray-les-Dunes. We drove along the roads to Furnes, but were brought up short, first by blown bridges, and then, on the main thoroughfare, by an incredible jam of lorries which were halted head to tail and three deep. In rear of this obstruction was a tank officer loudly announcing that he was on special duty and must be got through. For over an hour we worked hard to open even the narrowest of lanes. A general of division, whom we met by accident, wanted to know what I was doing there. Duly informed, he turned to with a will, and did, I must confess, a fine job. Our efforts were at last crowned with success. But it was too late for us to continue our journey. Even had we done so, what guarantee was there that we should not run into some other obstacle farther on? There was nothing for it but to beat a crestfallen retreat to Hondschoote.

We set out again at nightfall, this time on foot, and taking a more direct route. A pedestrian could scramble through where

17

a lorry would have been forced to a standstill. It was a hideous experience—or, at least, the last ten kilometres of the journey were. We had to make our way through an extraordinary confusion of motor traffic in a darkness that every minute was becoming more dense. The column was at Bray, right enough, and I was offered the hospitality of an empty house. Even a drink was forthcoming. Unfortunately—as the surgeons at the Zuydschoote hospital near by had only too good reason to know— the whole of the coastal district, bounded on the inland side by marshes and polders into which the salt had infiltrated, was almost completely without water, owing to the canals having been cut. We had nothing but champagne with which to quench our thirst. How gladly would I have exchanged mine for a chance of gulping my fill on the bank of some cool, clear river!

The Army, as such, having ceased to exist, I had no staff duties to perform. But I still had a 'cure of souls'. True, I no longer commanded a fuel depot, nor yet a detachment of mobile tanks. But I had worked for too long with these fine fellows to feel that I was justified in concentrating attention on my own affairs until I had done something to assure their future—which, in this instance—meant their embarkation. For no one was concerned to look farther ahead than that. The one thought in everybody's mind was to get clear of this damned stretch of coast before the enemy should smash through our last defences; to escape captivity by the sole road open to us—the sea. A sort of escape-hysteria had got hold of this mob of men. They were to all intents and purposes unarmed, and, from where they stood, packed together on the beaches, they could watch the English ahead of them already putting out to sea. I spent most of the 30th in trying to get my men's names on to the official evacuation lists. I went first to Bray-les-Dunes, which was chock-a-block with a disorderly crowd of soldiers searching for their units, and of lorries. Any man who happened to come along turned himself into a driver, only, very often, to abandon his chance vehicle after a few hundred yards. Once more I appointed myself Traffic-Control Officer, and tried, without much success, to get some kind of efficiency into the unfortunate Military Police who were clustered in ridiculous groups at every cross-roads. A little later I might have been seen at the 'Perroquet' café on the Belgian frontier, which, for a few hours, served as a temporary head-quarters for the Zone Commander. From there I went to Malo-les-Bains, where I found most of the 'Q' branch personnel. I spent that night bivouacking on the dunes. Our period of rest was punctuated by German shells. Fortunately, the enemy gunners, nothing if not methodical, concentrated on a point just to the left of the Malo-Terminus Hotel. The first salvoes claimed a number of victims. Thereafter the place was scrupulously avoided. If anyone had to pass near it, he did so at the run. Had the shooting been less accurate, what a scene of massacre there would have been in that sandy dormitory of ours among the sea-grasses!

Early next day I was assured that my men would be got on board. How could I have known that a bomb would sink their ship? Still, most of them, though not all, alas, were fished out of the water. I was free at last to think about myself. Our former second-in-command, who was still in charge, showed no very great eagerness to get his subordinates away before he himself was safe. He did, however, give me permission to make what arrangements I could. The phrase sounded ominous. Did it mean that I was to pull a fast one on some other unfortunate? Luckily, early that afternoon, the commander of the Cavalry Corps was kind enough to furnish me and two of my friends with an official movement-order. Nothing now remained but to find the ship to which we had been detailed.

As the result of a bungled message, the three of us were forced to go right through Dunkirk on two separate occasions, first from east to west, and then again in the reverse direction. I have a very vivid memory of the ruined town with its shells of buildings half-visible through drifting smoke, and its clutter, not of bodies but of human debris, in the streets. I can still hear the incredible din which, like the orchestral finale of an opera, provided an accompaniment to the last few minutes which we spent on the coast of Flanders—the crashing of bombs, the bursting of shells, the rat-tat-tat of machine-guns, the noise of anti-aircraft batteries, and, as a kind of figured bass, the persistent rattle of our own little naval pom-pom. But it is not the dangers and horrors of that day which have stuck most firmly in my memory. What comes back with especial clearness is our slow movement away from the jetty. A marvellous summer night shed its magic on the waters. The sky was pure gold, the sea a mirror, and the black, rank smoke, pouring from the burning refinery, made so lovely a pattern above the low shore-line that one was cheated into forgetting its tragic origin. Even the name painted on the stern of our vessel (*Royal Daffodil*) was like something out of an Indian fairy-tale. All things, as we slipped away, seemed to be in a conspiracy to accentuate the overwhelming and purely selfish feelings of relief which filled my mind as I thought of the prisoner's fate which I had so narrowly escaped.

We landed at Dover. Then came a whole day spent in travelling by train across southern England. That journey has left in my mind the memory of a sort of drugged exhaustion broken by chaotic sensations and images which, like the episodes of a dream, rose to the surface of my consciousness only to sink again almost immediately: the pleasure of devouring ham and cheese sandwiches handed through the windows by girls in multi-coloured dresses, and clergymen who looked as solemn as though they were administering the Sacrament; the faint, sweet smell of cigarettes showered on us with the same generous profusion; the acid taste of lemonade and the flat taste of tea with too much milk in it: the cosy green of lawns; a landscape made up of parks, cathedral spires, hedges, and Devonshire cliffs; groups of cheering children at level-crossings. But what struck us more than anything else was the warmth of our reception. 'How genuinely kind they are!' said my companions. Towards evening we re-embarked at Plymouth, and dropped anchor at dawn off Cherbourg. We had to wait a long time in the harbour. 'You see,' said the ship's officers (French this time), 'the dock officials don't get to their offices until nine.' We were back, alas, in the rear zones of a France at war. No more cheering crowds, no more sandwiches or cigarettes. We were given, on landing, a formal, dry, rather suspicious welcome. The rest camp was an inhospitable and squalid place brightened by the presence of a few ladies belonging to the Red Cross. Later still, after having been shaken to pieces in averagely uncomfortable railway carriages, we arrived in the middle of the night at Caen, where nobody seemed to be expecting us, but where, fortunately, we found a number of good hotels—and even bathrooms!

I shall have occasion at a later stage in this narrative of miseries to describe the efforts made to construct a serviceable fighting-force from the debris of an army, and to consider why the success achieved was so small. After remaining for some time in Normandy, we found ourselves finally stranded at Rennes. The First Army no longer existed. But Headquarters Staff, or what remained of it, was put at the disposition of the general commanding the 'Group' which had just been scraped together with the object, it was said, of defending Brittany. On 17 June Rennes was bombed from the air. We were stationed well outside the target zone, and if the sound of splintering glass caused by a direct hit, at some distance, on a dump of cheddite, made me wonder uneasily whether I might not be rather 'out' in my calculation of distances, these fears were quickly dissipated. 'How pleasant it is', says the Roman poet, 'to listen to a storm from the safe shelter of the shore.' The quotation is trite, the confession not altogether admirable. But what soldier, hearing the sounds of a danger from which he knows himself to be immune, is not conscious, deep in his heart, of a sense of purely animal relief?

On the morning of the 18th a rumour got about that the enemy was advancing. Our office was situated on one of the boulevards of the upper town. From the opposite side of the main street a road led downhill to the more populous district in which my batman was billeted. About eleven o'clock I went to tell him to get my things packed immediately. I was climbing the hill on my way back when, at the far end of the street, I saw a German column debouching on the boulevard. It was moving between me and my office. Not a shot was fired. A number of French soldiers, including a few officers, just stood and watched. I learned later that whenever the Germans came across a soldier still in possession of his arms, they merely made him smash his rifle and empty his ammunition pouches. I had long decided that I would take any step to avoid capture. Had I believed that I might, even now, be of the slightest use, I could, I hope, have screwed myself to the necessary pitch of courage to remain at my post. But now that all show of resistance had melted away, there was obviously no point in carrying on with my duties. Or, perhaps, I should put it this way: that it was more and more clearly borne in on me that the only manner in which I could continue to serve my country and my family was by escaping before the trap should finally be sprung.

It was obvious that if I tried to get away westwards—even assuming that any of the roads still remained open—I should merely get rounded up, sooner or later, in the cul-de-sac of the peninsula. If I went south there was a good chance that I should never get across the Loire. That, at least, was how I argued at the moment. I have since discovered that, contrary to my expectations, the Germans did not occupy Nantes until next day. But even had I tried that route, should I ever have succeeded in reaching the place? I also played with the idea of getting to Brest, where I might find some means of slipping across to

22

England. But should I have felt justified in abandoning my children and going into exile for an indefinite period? What, in fact, I did, after standing for a few moments deep in thought on the pavement of that hilly street, was to choose what seemed to me then the simplest, and, in the long run, the safest method of getting away. I went back to the house where I was billeted. There I took off my tunic. My rough serge trousers had nothing particularly military about them. From my landlord, who, with his son, showed, on this occasion, a high degree of courage, I got, without difficulty, the loan of a civilian jacket and tie. Then, after first making contact with an old friend who was a professor at Rennes, I booked a room in one of the hotels. Arguing that the best way to escape being noticed was to retain one's identity, I put my real name and occupation on the form handed to me by the manager. My grey hairs were sufficient guarantee that no one would suspect the presence of an army officer beneath the outward semblance of so obviously academic a figure—unless, of course, it occurred to the German authorities to check the hotel registers with the parade strength of the military formations known to be in the neighbourhood. Such a course seems never to have entered their heads. No doubt our masters were already beginning to feel a bit blasé on the subject of prisoners.

In this way I spent about a fortnight at Rennes. I was constantly running up against German officers in the streets, in restaurants, and even in my hotel. My mind was torn between the agony of seeing the cities of my native land given over to the invader, a sense of surprise at finding myself on peaceful terms with men whom, a few days earlier, I should never have dreamed of encountering save at the revolver's point, and the malicious pleasure of pulling a fast one on these gentlemen without their having the slightest suspicion that I was doing anything of the sort. Not that this satisfaction was wholly unmixed. I have always felt a certain discomfort in living under false pretences, and though, in this case, I feel sure that my conduct would have passed muster with the strictest of casuists, I could not help feeling amazement at the determination with which I continued to play my part. As soon as the railways were running again, I went to Angers, where I had a number of friends, and thence, by road, to Guéret and my family. Of the delights of this home-coming I shall say nothing. To speak of them would set my heart beating too fast. It is better to draw over them a curtain of silence.

The reader will have gathered from what I have said, how limited was the nature of my experience—experience, I mean, of *this* war, since the former one comes into the picture only in so far as it provides a general background. I lived and worked at a fairly high staff level. True, I did not always know everything that was going on. Very often, as I shall hope to show, I was left without information essential to the proper performance of my duties. But, as a result of my daily routine, I was in a position to draw my own conclusions about both men and methods. On the other hand, I had no first-hand experience of fighting, and my contacts with the front-line troops were few and far between. In my references to them I have been compelled to rely on the evidence of others, which I was conveniently placed to collect and sift. I feel justified, therefore, in putting certain of my reflections on record, though nothing can really ever take the place of seeing things with one's own eyes—provided one is blest with good sight. By relying on second-hand evidence one is bound to lose something of the truth and much of the human atmosphere. But no man exists who can claim to have witnessed everything at first-hand, or to have had all the knowledge available. The most we can ask is that each shall say frankly what he has to say. From a comparison of particular sincerities, truth will eventually emerge.

Chapter Two

ONE OF THE VANQUISHED GIVES
EVIDENCE

WE have just suffered such a defeat as no one would have believed possible. On whom or on what should the blame be laid? On the French system of parliamentary government, say our generals; on the rank and file of the fighting services, on the English, on the fifth column—in short, on any and everybody except themselves. Old Joffre was wiser. 'Whether I was responsible for the winning of the Battle of the Marne', he said, 'I do not know. But of this I feel pretty certain, that, had it been lost, the failure would have been laid at my door.' He intended, by that remark, to remind us that a commanding officer is responsible for everything that happens while he is in supreme charge of events. Whether the initiative for each separate decision comes directly from him, whether in each instance he knows what is being done, is beside the point. The mere fact that he has accepted the position of 'Chief' means that he must take upon his shoulders the burden of failure as well as the panoply of success. The great truth which that simple man expressed so unequivocally is seen to-day to have an even deeper meaning. When the Army was disbanded after the final campaign, it would have been hard to find a single officer among those with whom I was in daily contact who had the slightest doubt on the subject. Whatever the deep-seated causes of the disaster may have been, the immediate occasion (as I shall attempt to explain later) was the utter incompetence of the High Command.[1]

---

[1] Let me support this statement by quoting a remark made by General Weygand, who was at one time Director of the School of Advanced Military Studies, and, later, Commander-in-Chief. It was made on 25 May 1940 (*Secret Documents of the French General Staff*, p. 140). '. . . France committed the capital error of

One of the Vanquished gives Evidence

I very much fear that this brutally frank assertion may shock many in whose minds certain prejudices are deeply rooted. Almost the whole of our national Press, and the more academic portions of our national literature, have, as I see it, consistently upheld the conventional view in these matters. For a great many journalists and for a considerable number of 'patriotic' authors, any general is, by definition, a *great* general. If he leads his men to disaster, he is duly rewarded with a high class of the Legion of Honour. No doubt the argument runs that only by drawing a decent veil over the more glaring indiscretions of our public men can the morale of the country be kept at a high level. In fact, the only result of this method is to sow the seeds of a dangerous irritation in the minds of those who make up the fighting forces. But there are other motives, too; some of them, perhaps, not quite so discreditable.

A somewhat odd historical law seems to control the relations existing between States and their military chiefs. Successful soldiers are almost always kept from exercising any political power, though the failures receive it as a free gift from the hands of those very citizens whom they have been unable to lead to victory. MacMahon in spite of Sedan, Hindenburg after the collapse of 1918, were both chosen to preside over the régimes which emerged from defeat. It is not the Pétain of Verdun or the Weygand of Rethondes whom France to-day has promoted or accepted. I realize, of course, that recent events did not result wholly from a spontaneous movement of the popular will. Still, they do stand in some sort of relation to what is, in effect, a form of collective psychosis. In the eyes of the defeated, uniforms bristling with badges of rank and smothered in decorations symbolize not only sacrifices willingly endured on the field of battle, but also the glories of our past and, quite possibly, of our future. When a widely held opinion is glaringly at odds

entering this war without the necessary material, and without that basis of military theory which alone could have led to success. . . .' (July 1942.)

26

with the truth, we are bound in honesty, I think, to attack it.
I share Pascal's view that 'it is a very strange kind of enthusiasm
that is roused to fury against those who point out the errors of
our public men, rather than against the men themselves . . .'.
'The Saints', he writes elsewhere, 'have never kept silent.' It
is not my intention to use the phrase as a general justification for
every kind of fault-finding. Nevertheless, it should be carefully
pondered by all who—without, alas, being able to lay claim to
sanctity—try to govern their lives by the standards of the normal
decent man. Those who genuinely respect these will find that it
is impossible, with an easy conscience, to avoid doing their duty.

I referred a while back to the 'High Command'. But scarcely
had my pen written the words than the historian in me was
shocked by their use. For the ABC of my trade consists in
avoiding big-sounding abstract terms. Those who teach history
should be continually concerned with the task of seeking the
solid and the concrete behind the empty and the abstract. In
other words, it is on men rather than functions that they should
concentrate their attention. The errors of the High Command
were, fundamentally, the errors of a specific group of human
beings.

I have had little to do with the men at the top. Both my
junior rank and the nature of my duties kept me at a distance from
them. The only one with whom I had occasional dealings of a
kind that might be called in any degree intimate was General
Blanchard. My chief memory of him is that of a man whose outstanding characteristic was 'good breeding'. The last time he
honoured me with a few words was when we met in Normandy
just after I had got back from Flanders. On that occasion he
said, in tones of kindly interest: 'So you, too, managed to get
out of that adventure with a whole skin?' The phrase hardly
seemed, I must confess, altogether suited to the occasion. Félix,
in the last scene of *Polyeucte*, is guilty of much the same sort of
inappropriate remark when he says '*Bénissons notre heureuse*

aventure!'—on which Voltaire makes the following comment: 'It is hard to keep from laughing when a man who has just cut his son-in-law's throat speaks like that!' Blanchard's own part in the Flanders 'adventure' had been to lose more than half his army, and to abandon not only his own Chief of Staff, but the officer whom he had himself nominated as his successor, both of whom had stood their ground though perfectly well aware that they would be captured. I know that one should never judge a man on the evidence of a single piece of ill-luck. But one morning, when we were at the Château of Attiches, I was called to the telephone very early to speak to British G.H.Q. On that occasion I spent more than an hour in the same room as the general. During all that time he sat in tragic immobility, saying nothing, doing nothing, but just gazing at the map spread on the table between us, as though hoping to find on it the decision which he was incapable of taking. At Attiches, too, I quite accidentally overheard him say something which amazed me at the time, and about which I shall have some remarks to make later. On the whole, however, my knowledge of him was confined to the orders that he issued, and I find it difficult, where they are concerned, to distinguish between what he did on his own initiative and what he was persuaded to do by his staff.

I was, naturally enough, very much more familiar with the officers who were my immediate seniors or my colleagues. Most of them were regulars who had been through the Staff College. So well did I know them that I must resist the temptation to paint what would be a highly personal composite portrait of the 'Staff Officer Type'. When I shut my eyes and rummage among the memories of the past, I see a long line of sharply differentiated individuals. Some of them are just figures of fun. Others will remain dear to me for as long as I live. There was, for instance, Captain B . . . of 'G' branch, who moved with his empty head for ever in the clouds. Like a priest at the Elevation, he seemed to spend his time in administering to a crowd of worshippers the book-knowledge which he had absorbed in the course of endless peace-time manœuvres. Then there was Captain X..., a former fellow-officer in the regiment, whose mouth spoke louder than his actions. Like so many regulars, he seemed to regard it as his especial duty to keep his juniors 'in their place', with the result that, after a few months, he was thoroughly hated by the lot of us. How we laughed each time he went off to spend the night in a deep dug-out! Very different from such fire-eaters was that dear mess-companion of ours who was always ready with a helping hand, who never paraded his courage, and who performed with such unostentatious efficiency the duties which fell to him first as adjutant to our immediate chief, and later as liaison officer. Against him I have only one serious charge to bring. He was too easily discouraged. As a result, perhaps, of physical fatigue, or perhaps because he saw his dreams of what war ought to be, crumble in the harsh air of reality, he let himself be quite unnecessarily captured one evening after a gruelling time at Steenwerck. To do that was, in itself, a proof of terrible mental suffering, and even worse was in store for him when news of the armistice reached him through the medium of a German newspaper.

We had, from the days of Bohain on, plenty of opportunity to gauge the value of the men I have mentioned, but the heat of battle brought many a revelation—not always of the kind we might have expected.

Take, for instance, the case of that senior officer who had emerged from the war of 1914 with an imposing array of decorations. We were well placed in advance to know his good qualities—which were not lacking in charm—and also of his bad ones, which were of formidable dimensions. He had a sense of reality, though with it went a lack of mental discipline. He was endowed with a gift of 'muddling through', but showed a mulish dislike of planning ahead. He was pleasant in his dealings with colleagues or inferiors, but not seldom lacking in frankness.

None of us, however, could possibly have foreseen the way in which he completely went to pieces when faced by the imperatives of action. Looking back on what happened, and speaking quite frankly, I cannot help feeling now that we may have been a bit unfair in our attitude to him. I am afraid that, without ever really giving the matter much thought, we rather crudely attributed to weakness in the face of danger what—though it had all the outward symptoms of fear—was probably due in the main to an almost prophetic awareness of the catastrophe hanging over our heads. To make matters worse, he was cursed with an excess of sensibility, and knew that the load he had to carry was too heavy for him. He told me himself, at Attiches, that the duty of detailing those members of the staff who were to remain with the advanced elements was more than he could face. But one thing is certain. Weighed down, I do not doubt, by years spent in office work and conditioned by a purely academic training, this regular soldier had lost every quality of leadership—and of the self-control and ruthlessness which the word implies.

Turning to the other panel of the diptych, how can I resist the temptation to evoke for memory's eye that tall fair-haired captain of gunners who, when things at Attiches and at Steenwerck were at their worst, took over command of our Advanced H.Q.? Earlier, at Bohain, where he had been in charge of supplies, we had thought him fussy and a bit given to eyewash. He was not particularly quick-witted, and, as a bred-in-the-bone cavalryman, never ceased to announce his dislike of brain-work. We could not help respecting the way in which he would maintain any opinion in which he believed through thick and thin, even in the teeth of his superiors, though we found his spirit of contradiction decidedly irritating. His—perhaps rather deliberately assumed—liking for scatological humour soon wearied even the least squeamish among us. His prejudices—political, social (he came from the upper middle-class), and, presumably, racial—were as alien to my own outlook as they possibly could

30

be. Still, we got along perfectly well together, though neither of us, I fear, showed any special warmth of affection for the other.

Then came the campaign of the Nord. When the end could no longer be in doubt, General Prioux decided that each H.Q. section should nominate an officer to stay with him until the enemy arrived. T . . . , as I have already said, was at that time in charge of our office. He maintained that the fact of his holding such a position made it impossible for him to ask anybody else to take on a job which meant inevitable self-sacrifice. But he was strong-minded, and did not hold that the acceptance of an unnecessary captivity was any part of an honourable soldier's duty. What he planned was something quite different. As he has since told me in confidence, he spent that last night with his eye glued to a hole in the hedge, intending to jump out on the Germans revolver in hand. And he would most certainly have been as good as his word had not something occurred unexpectedly at the last moment to restore his liberty of movement. During the night the Commander of the Fourth Corps suddenly appeared at Advanced H.Q. It had become clear that none of the units in his formation would be able to re-cross the Lys, and he had therefore decided to throw in his lot with that of the Army Commander. Naturally, he was accompanied by his liaison officer, who turned out to be a member of our own mess. The poor fellow refused, as I have already explained, to take advantage of this opportunity to reach the coast, and this attitude of unselfishness, though it was the outcome of excessive exhaustion, saved T. . . . The general had asked each section to detail one officer who would remain behind and be taken prisoner. T . . . was given permission to leave. Next morning we were surprised and delighted to see him appear, punctual almost to the dot, at our first rendezvous, which was not far from Hondschoote, riding a brand-new bicycle which he had picked up in the course of his journey in one of the deserted streets of Bailleul.

Next evening we said good-bye to one another in an

31

atmosphere of considerable, if suppressed, emotion. If we did not admit in so many words that we had previously been quite wrong in our mutual attitude and deeply regretted it, that is because such things are usually left unspoken. It was enough that we should both feel as we did. Since then, the accidents of the times have so completely separated us that I have no idea as I write these lines whether he is still alive. If we ever do meet again, I have a horrid feeling that we shall once more find ourselves at odds: but not in quite the old way. I, certainly, shall find it impossible to forget those few moments, so charged with personal electricity, which we passed in one another's company in a garden at Steenwerck or the period which led up to, and was conditioned by, them. It is one of the privileges of the true man of action that, when the critical moment comes, blemishes of character are effaced, while virtues, till then potential merely, are seen in an unexpectedly vivid light. Of this metamorphosis our friend gave an unexpected and outstanding example. He had always been both conscientious and sincere. Faced by a genuine test, his preoccupation with trivialities ceased to operate, and his spirit of contradiction vanished. Always ready to instruct and to direct, he was the type of leader who knows how to leave to his subordinates that freedom of action which is so necessary if they are to carry out his orders effectively, though he never attempted to shuffle out of his ultimate responsibility for them. He was patient and calm no matter how desperate the situation might be, and, if he refused to accept physical exhaustion in others as an excuse for failure, would himself work till he dropped. And what a good fellow he was! Knowing him, I feel that I have known one really great man.

But in every human group there is something over and above the individuals who compose it, and the more clearly defined the community to which they belong, the more do their own characteristics become blurred. Similarity of training, professional routine, and the need to submit to the rules and regulations of a common way of life are not, in themselves, enough to hold a group together. What is needed is something more than a tradition handed down by seniors to juniors, by leaders to subordinates; it is an *esprit de corps*. This is particularly true in the case of military organizations. Within the body of the nation the officers of the regular army form a separate and distinct society. Embodying, as it does, a number of habits and attitudes which are survivals from an earlier age, it is peculiarly suited to restore, in the general dead level of modern life, that idea of 'hierarchy' which was never, in our older France, completely identical with 'class'. The members of the nobility always, in spite of great differences of blood, had a very definite idea of basic equality. So strong was this sense, in fact, that the sovereign, *qua man*, was looked upon as being no more than the 'first gentleman of his kingdom'. Similarly, to-day, if a general officer, no matter how senior his rank, entering a room where a junior officer was working, were to fail to shake hands with him, he would be considered to have offended against the most elementary rules of good behaviour. On the other hand, if the man he saw there was—I won't say a private, but an N.C.O.—he would do so only in the most exceptional circumstances. Within the military hierarchy again, the world of staff officers forms a remarkably homogeneous whole, having many clearly marked characteristics. Of these, the most honourable is undoubtedly its strong sense of professional duty, though this it shares, I am quite sure, with all officers of the regular army no matter what their rank. No doubt there are among the graduates of the Staff College—as elsewhere—idlers and irresponsibles, but except in one instance I have never met them, and the individual who was the exception referred to had quite obviously been summed up by his colleagues and sent to vegetate in a staff job of very minor importance. It is hard to overestimate this particular virtue, and it is a pity that other branches of the national service do not possess it to a similar degree.

One of the Vanquished gives Evidence

There has been much talk about the contempt shown for the regimental officer by his opposite number on the staff. I do not deny that there may be a number of conceited individuals who show an irritating Staff-College mentality, but the species is, on the whole, a rare one. It is only fair to say that all the staff officers with whom I have had dealings were extremely anxious (or said they were) to return to regimental duties. No doubt it was the 'smart' attitude to take, and their eloquence may have owed not a little to snobbery. Some I have known who showed a much-diminished enthusiasm when they had 'their backs to the wall'. Still, my own feeling is that in the vast majority of cases—especially among the younger men—this feeling was perfectly genuine. However that may be, it is not a little significant that such a peculiar form of snobbery should have come to exist at all, and that it should be a matter of 'good form' to express admiration for, and envy of, the front-line formations.

Misunderstandings are bound to occur at times in all armies, no matter what their nationality, between administrative and executive services. But it is not always the former who are responsible. Problems look different according to the angle from which they are observed, and those whose functions are not the same can hardly be expected to see eye to eye. The 'thinking oneself into the other fellow's shoes' is always a very difficult form of mental gymnastics, and it is not confined to men who occupy a special position in the military hierarchy. But it would be foolish to deny that staff officers as a whole have been a good deal to blame in this matter of sympathetic understanding. Their failure, when they did fail, was, however, due—I feel pretty sure—not so much to contempt as to lack of imagination and a tendency to take refuge from the urgency of fact in abstractions. In the days before the real fighting had begun, we spent a lot of time working out troop movements on the map. But how many of us ever adequately realized what problems of detail, what frictions of psychology, are involved when, in the depth of winter, men are asked to leave billets in which they have settled down and move somewhere else into what are, only too often, bad and unsuitable quarters? But that is not the worst of the staff's shortcomings. More than once during the First World War it was brought home to me how inefficient the High Command could be when it came to calculating accurately the length of time needed for an order, once issued from H.Q., to pass through its various recipients until finally it reached the formations who would have to act upon it. No amount of 'instructions' will ever succeed in convincing the unimaginative that a runner's pace is slow, and that he will often go wrong when roads and tracks have been turned into a sea of mud. On 22 July 1918 I was serving with Mangin's Army—in which the methods of inter-communication were particularly unsatisfactory. On one occasion I was appalled to receive for re-transmission an order to attack at such short notice that it was impossible to get it to the troops concerned in time. They were actually already on the move. When it did arrive, it was so late that the battalion detailed to carry it out had no opportunity to reconnoitre the ground before daylight, advanced to the assault on a wrong bearing, and was slaughtered almost to a man, quite uselessly. I am not at all sure that the conduct of the Second World War was entirely free from similar mistakes. The blame for them falls, not on individuals, but on the whole method of training in vogue at the time. This is a subject to which I shall return later.

One simple and obvious remedy for this state of affairs would have been to establish a system which would have made it possible for small groups of officers to serve, turn and turn about, in the front line and at H.Q. But senior generals dislike having the personnel of their staffs changed too often. It should be remembered that in 1915 and 1916 their opposition to any reform along these lines led to an almost complete divorce between the outlook of the regimental and the staff officer. When, finally, it was found to be impossible to go on any longer in the old way,

35

the necessary changes had been too long delayed, with the result that transfers had to be made on far too large a scale. By that time, too, our heavy losses had made it almost impossible to provide a sufficient number of officers suited to fill H.Q. appointments. It does not follow that a good company or battalion commander will be a good staff officer. It made me very uneasy to see, during the winter of 1939–40, that the old system of watertight compartments was once again in the ascendant. I did my best to point out its inherent dangers to those in high places, but the crisis of the following May and June developed so quickly that the bad effects were not fully felt.

Honest, markedly anxious to do their best, deeply patriotic, and, for the most part, a great deal less mentally hide-bound than the technicians and the regular officers from whom they are recruited, at times, even, genuinely brilliant, the members of the General Staff do, generally speaking, form a body of men who are deserving of the highest esteem. Still, it cannot be denied that, by their own actions, or by those of the generals drawn from their number, they did lead us to defeat. Why was this? Before I attempt to answer that question I had better first describe how this unfortunate result came about.

I make no claim to be writing a critical history of the war, or even of the campaign of the Nord. I have not had access to any of the documents necessary for such an undertaking, nor do I possess the requisite technical knowledge. But there are certain obvious facts which should be made clear without further delay.

What drove our armies to disaster was the cumulative effect of a great number of different mistakes. One glaring characteristic is, however, common to all of them. Our leaders, or those who acted for them, were incapable of thinking in terms of a *new* war. In other words, the German triumph was, essentially, a triumph of intellect—and it is that which makes it so peculiarly serious.

Let me be more precise. One fact, but that one of radical importance, differentiates our contemporary civilization from any of those that preceded it. Since the beginning of the twentieth century the whole idea of distance has changed. This alteration in spatial values came about in little more than a single generation. But rapid though it was, it has become so much a part of our mental habit that we are inclined to forget how revolutionary its effects have been. What is happening to-day may serve to open our eyes. The privations resulting from war and defeat have had upon Europe the repercussions of a Time Machine in reverse. We have been plunged suddenly into a way of life which, only quite recently, we thought had disappeared for ever. I am writing these lines in my house in the country. A year ago, when I and the local tradesmen had all the petrol we needed, the county town, on which the economic life of the district centres, seemed close at hand. Now, when bicycles are the quickest means of transport available, and heavy loads have to be carried in donkey-wagons, every trip to market becomes a major expedition. We have gone back thirty or forty years! The ruling idea of the Germans in the conduct of this war was speed. We, on the other hand, did our thinking in terms of yesterday or the day before. Worse still: faced by the undisputed evidence of Germany's new tactics, we ignored, or wholly failed to understand, the quickened rhythm of the times. So true is this, that it was as though the two opposed forces belonged, each of them, to an entirely different period of human history. We interpreted war in terms of assagai *versus* rifle made familiar to us by long years of colonial expansion. But this time it was we who were cast for the rôle of the savage![1]

[1] Much intelligent comment on this question of increased speed, and on its effects on thought, is to be found in a small book which few would dream of consulting—Charlesworth's *Trade-Routes and Commerce of the Roman Empire.* See, for instance, what the author says on p. 225, and especially this: 'Men have to be flurried and worried to adjust their minds to a celerity of decision at which our grandfathers would have gasped.' (July 1942.)

One of the Vanquished gives Evidence

Read over again the list of places where the First Army established its headquarters during the campaign of the Nord: Valenciennes, Douai, Lens, Estaires, Attiches, Steenwerck. Each time the enemy exerted pressure there was a withdrawal. This was only to be expected. But what was the extent of these withdrawals? The average was between 20 and 30 kilometres, never more than 30. In other words—remembering Vidal de la Blanche's aphorism that the time taken in covering a given distance, rather than the distance itself, is what matters to-day—approximately half an hour's run by car. Naturally, the movement of the defensive line was strictly related to that of headquarters, and corresponded to such limitation of advance as the High Command thought it could impose upon the enemy. At our school-house in Lens we were well within earshot of machine-gun fire. The old soldiers of 1914 might well feel inclined to draw comparisons when they remembered how seldom such sounds had reached the back areas in those days. I can hardly believe that our leaders were solely actuated by a desire to give their staffs this particular form of treat! The truth of the matter was that the Germans advanced a great deal faster than they should have done according to the old rules of the game. And so it went on. 'Niggling' was how I heard our strategic methods described by a colleague of mine, one of those younger men who did at least know how to think in contemporary terms, and suffered under a perpetual sense of frustration because of the way in which they were consistently ignored by their superiors. One could, however, fully realize a situation, the nature of which was only too clear, without having worn out the seat of one's pants on the benches of the Staff College or of the C.H.E.M. (*Centre des Hautes Études Militaires*). It was perfectly obvious that as soon as the Army of the Meuse had been broken, and the enemy began to show signs of becoming active on our front, the only hope of re-establishing the general situation lay in our 'disengaging', and establishing a new defensive line sufficiently far

38

back to ensure that it would not be overrun before it had been properly organized. But nothing of the sort was done. Instead, small groups of reinforcements were continually dribbled into every breach as it occurred, with the inevitable result that they were cut to pieces. At the same time our masters showed a mulish determination to maintain a salient in the direction of Valenciennes and Denain, the only consequence of which was that, when finally it was decided to retreat to the coast, the divisions left to hold these advanced positions could not be withdrawn in time. If Joffre had behaved like that after Charleroi and Maubeuge, he would never have won the Marne That battle would have developed, instead, somewhere in the direction of Guise, and he would have lost it. Remember, too, that in his day opposing armies moved only on foot.

I do not pretend to know on which of the various commands—First Army, G.H.Q., or First Army Group (which held a sort of middle position)—the main responsibility for these mistakes rested. The Army Group was at first under General Billotte who, after 25 May, was replaced by General Blanchard. Billotte was mortally injured in a car smash on the 21st, and cannot, therefore, speak in his own defence. His convenient disappearance from the scene led to his being cast for the rôle of scapegoat, and, to judge from the odds and ends of gossip which I picked up in our gloomy little mess-room at Malo-les-Bains, his colleagues were only too glad to let him play it for all it was worth.

There can be no doubt that our whole plan of campaign was wrong. What *should* have been the reply of the Anglo-French forces to the German invasion of Belgium? The problem had been discussed all through the winter by the various 'G' staffs. Two solutions, among many others, found particular favour. One school of thought maintained that we ought to stand on a line in Belgium based at its northern end on the Escaut, with its eastern resting on the (unfortunately incomplete) system of blockhouses and anti-tank ditches which roughly followed the line of the frontier. Forward elements were to be given the duty of reconnoitring and fighting a delaying action. The other school favoured immediate offensive action *across* the frontier, and, with that intention, proposed that, as soon as the Germans moved, we should advance to, and occupy, the left bank of the Dyle and of the Belgian Meuse, with the forces between these two points spread out along a diagonal lying from Wavre to Namur across the high plateau of Hesbaye which is almost entirely devoid of natural obstacles. As everybody knows, it was this second plan that ultimately carried the day, and it seems fairly certain that General Billotte's personal influence was decisive in imposing this decision.

The choice was, probably, in any case an unfortunate one. It certainly became so once the Belgian resistance round Liége began to crumble. We had been relying on a respite of several days in which to man and organize our new front. The failure to destroy the bridges between Liége and Maastricht, as planned, meant that the position was turned almost at the outset of the German offensive. The reports received from Intelligence made it pretty clear that it must collapse pretty soon. Nor was that all. Our first encounters with the enemy had produced a number of unpleasant surprises.

Not only were the German tanks a great deal more numerous than Intelligence had led us to suppose: some of them were quite unexpectedly powerful. The extent to which our Air Force was outclassed was truly appalling. The job of making contact to the east of the Dyle and the Wavre–Namur line had been entrusted to the Cavalry Corps. This, in spite of its traditional title, was entirely motorized—'the only formation with which I have never had anything to do', the Army Veterinary Officer said to me one day. General Prioux, who at that time was in command of this strong concentration of troops, proposed on the 11th that the whole plan should be abandoned, and the line at once withdrawn to the Escaut and the French frontier. Once again, Billotte intervened. When an officer of such exalted rank takes the trouble to play a part in strategic decisions, it is rarely, indeed, that he does not carry the day. I have good reason for believing that Prioux, after an interview with the Group Commander, agreed at least to modify his memorandum. However that may be, it was, in the event, completely ignored.

What, I wonder, would have happened to our First Army and to the Anglo-French forces on its left, if the yawning gap on the Meuse had not, contrary to all expectation, suddenly developed on its right flank? I do not feel competent to commit myself to any prophecy after the event. On 14 May a section of our front was broken. It had been held by a Moroccan division. The native troops of which it was composed seem, at first, anyhow, to have stood up very badly to aerial bombardment and tanks. But the line was re-established pretty quickly.

There can be no doubt whatever that it was the collapse of the Armies of the Meuse and at Sedan which, by uncovering the rear of the troops engaged in Belgium, led to the complete failure of the entire scheme. How came it that the sharply escarped valley of a large river, which everybody had regarded as providing an ideal defensive position, was, in fact, so badly held? Up till now I have succeeded in gathering only a few contradictory rumours bearing on this incident which was one of the most important and, perhaps, surprising, of the whole war. But I do know, only too well, that the High Command was lamentably slow in learning its lessons.

On 13 May we were informed that the line of the Meuse had been broken. On the very same day, an order, signed by Gamelin, was issued to the effect that resistance must be maintained on the Wavre–Namur position. Not until the 15th was it decided to begin a general movement of withdrawal, and even then, as I have already had occasion to note, the operation was carried out in a very piecemeal fashion. No alteration whatever was brought about in these methods either by the replacement of Gamelin by Weygand (which took place on the 20th) or by the call next day which the new Commander-in-Chief set out to make on Lord Gort and General Billotte.[1] This highly dramatic journey had to be made by air, because land communications were already disrupted as far north as the coast. It was on his way back from this expedition that the Army Group Commander, who always, it was said, drove at breakneck speed, crashed into a lorry. What precisely had been the part played by this officer in the events of the 13th onwards? I have no special information on the point. But one thing is certain: the errors committed at that time had results out of all proportion to their cause. In themselves they were a great deal less unforgivable than was the initial plan of campaign—for all its seeming dash and brilliance. After all, many great soldiers have started off on the wrong foot. Early mistakes become tragic only when the men in charge are incapable of putting them right. Billotte's disappearance from the scene might have led men to suppose that a new wind would begin to blow at headquarters. But such was not the case. That he had faults no one would dream of denying, but it seems probable that they were not peculiar to him, but were common to the whole school of thought which he represented.

The campaign of the Nord taught us a number of hard lessons. Can one say that they did, at least, convince our masters that the whole rhythm of modern warfare had changed its tempo? The answer to that question is to be found in the final convulsions which engulfed the remnants which succeeded in escaping from the disasters of the Flemish theatre. The ships which had enabled us to avoid captivity threw upon the coast of France a confused medley of elements disorganized by retreat, by the

---

[1] I give the story as it was told me at the time. If my memory of Weygand's Report to the Anglo-French War Council on the 22nd (*Secret Documents of the French General Staff*, p. 130) is correct, he never, in fact, succeeded in making contact with Lord Gort. (July 1942.)

chaotic conditions of their embarkation, and by, in some cases, actual shipwreck. They were without arms of any kind. Whole units had to be sorted out, reorganized, and completely re-equipped. For this delicate and necessarily slow operation the High Command chose a tract of country which barely extended from Evreux to Caen. The Somme front, which was still fluid, lay on an average no more than 150 kilometres distant. That would have been more than enough in the days of Napoleon: it would have been adequate even in 1915: in the year of grace 1940 it amounted to just nothing at all. The Germans soon left us in no doubt of that. We were compelled, almost at once, to withdraw in a southerly direction, at first, following our usual custom, only a few miles, but later, very much farther. But by then the final disaster had already begun to take shape. Actually, we should have been taken down to the Charente, if not to the Garonne, for regrouping; to some area, that is, where we should have been well placed for a move in any direction. Had that been done we might still have been in a position to make our-selves felt. I feel as bitterly angry when I think of it to-day as I did in those successive Norman châteaux between which we moved. Nor were we the only victims—or even the most to be pitied—of an astonishing thick-headedness which consistently refused to draw the obvious conclusions. The Germans advanc-ing towards the plains of the Saône, the Jura, and the Rhine were given ample time in which to surround the French Armies of the East, and almost to surround the Army of the Alps. From the beginning to the end of the war, the metronome at headquarters was always set at too slow a beat. One particular incident, which was significant though not, in itself, of any great practical importance, served me as proof that this curious form of mental sclerosis was not confined to those senior members of the hierarchy who were to blame for having withdrawn us for re-grouping no farther than the area immediately behind the front. When the task of carrying out this reorganization was at last,

after much shilly-shallying, entrusted to the General Commanding the 16th Corps, the staff of the First Army, which had nothing
to do and was in thoroughly bad odour with the authorities,
found itself immobilized in the area south of Caen, where its
members occupied two small country houses. At last, on 15 June,
we received orders to report to Rennes. The journey was to be
made partly by rail, partly by road. The number of cars available
was small, and in the early stages of the move what there were
were used to take the train-parties to the station. By evening this
shuttle service had been concluded and I set off with a friend to
find the lieutenant-colonel who was the highest-ranking officer
on the spot. Our object was to convince him of the necessity of
getting us started as soon as possible. Everyone knew that
German motorized columns were infiltrating into Normandy,
and that they were, in particular, threatening our communications with the south. A consignment of officers, unarmed except
for a few revolvers, would have made a poor showing in the
event of a surprise encounter with mobile machine-gunners.
There was considerable risk that we might, quite unnecessarily,
find ourselves captured in the very act of withdrawing, and such
a prospect was, to say the least, extremely unpopular. The
lieutenant-colonel began his usual humming and ha'ing, but the
idea of arriving at Rennes after dark, and of being exposed to a
good deal of inconvenience as a result, finally decided him to
postpone breaking camp until the early hours of the next morning. Truth obliges me to confess that, as things turned out, this
delay had no ill effects. The fact remains, however, that it
represented the height of imprudence, and its occurrence inclines
me to believe that there may have been more truth than is
popularly allowed in the story of the still higher ranking officer
who, dining at ease on the banks of the Oise, suddenly found
himself surrounded by a party of *feldgrau*.

Did we ever, really, in the whole course of the campaign
know the precise location of the enemy at any given time? That

44

our commanders should have had a very imperfect idea of his intentions, and, worse still, of his material resources, can easily be explained by the faulty organization of our Intelligence Service. But the fact that we were never quite certain of his movements was due mainly to a persistent failure ever to judge distances correctly. Our own rate of progress was too slow and our minds were too inelastic for us ever to admit the possibility that the enemy might move with the speed which he actually achieved. When we left Lens on 22 June, H.Q. was split into two sections—an 'advanced' group at Estaires, with a less mobile organization at Merville, where it was thought that it would be at a safe distance from the theatre of operations. What was our surprise when it was borne in upon us that, in fact, the so-called 'rear' H.Q. was a great deal closer to the line than its advanced brother! When the Germans crashed through the Meuse defences, we were compelled to improvise at short notice alternative rail-heads for the division which we were preparing to rush into the lion's mouth in the hope of blocking egress from the pocket.

After our arrival in Flanders there was a marked increase in the number of such miscalculations. On one occasion a divisional commander, making his way to the map-reference at which it had been decided to establish his headquarters, found that he had been anticipated by the enemy. I still have an unpleasant feeling in the pit of my stomach when I remember one tragic incident which I very nearly precipitated—in all innocence, let me add, since I had no means of appreciating the situation, and was not to blame if the information available to other members of the staff had not been passed on to me in time to be utilized. I had arranged to move one of my mobile fuel-supply companies farther back, to some point where it would be less dangerously within striking distance of our eastern front. The necessary orders had already gone out when I learned that the Germans, advancing from the *south-west*, had already occupied the village for which my men were making. By a miracle the column was held up in a traffic jam, and never arrived. Part of a motor-transport group, however, was less fortunate. As it was approaching the outskirts of the town which had been allotted to it by Army H.Q. as its billeting area, it was met by heavy-machine-gun fire. Every man jack of its personnel was either killed or taken prisoner.

Shall I ever forget, finally, how the news reached us that the French section of our road to the sea was on the point of being cut? Lachamp and I had, already, some days earlier, evacuated most of our fuel park to a camp at no great distance from the coast. One by one our permanent depots had all been overrun until we could depend only on those in the immediate neighbourhood of Lille. When we were lucky enough to find a few odd railway trucks loaded with petrol tins, we thought it simpler to let the various units take what they wanted without more ado. Consequently, our servicing staff had practically nothing to occupy them. We had with us only one small detachment of fighting troops, and a number of officers most of whom were employed in keeping open our communications with the various corps. Meanwhile the Army, now in full retreat, was concentrating in an area which grew daily more constricted, so constricted in fact that the different Corps H.Q. were finally situated so close to one another that we could easily visit all of them in a couple of trips or so. It seemed to us, therefore, the merest common sense not to expose to the risk of capture any more officers than were strictly necessary. On the evening of the 26th we decided to send one of these officers to make contact with the main body of our supply personnel. In the course of the morning of the 28th he returned to Steenwerck. It appeared that at some point between Steenwerck and Cassel, on the road that he had been told to take, he had run into a detachment of enemy tanks. This was serious news, and I at once passed on the information to my superiors. 'Are you quite sure that they weren't *French* tanks?' asked the first member of 'G' branch whom we saw. F . . . replied that he had every reason to think they were not, since there had been an exchange of shots between their crews and our own troops. General Prioux, to whom we next took him, was less incredulous, and received the news without batting an eyelid. But I still cannot help wondering how long we should have had to wait for this piece of intelligence if our friend the lieutenant had not been lucky enough to be just on the spot at the right moment.

But it would not be fair to confine these criticisms to the High Command. Generally speaking, the combatant troops were no more successful than the staff in adjusting their movements or their tactical appreciations to the speed at which the Germans moved. But failure in either case sprang from much the same causes. Not only was the passing on of information extremely inefficient, whether it emanated from lower or higher formations, but the front-line officers, though less highly trained, had, most of them, passed through the same process of professional education as their colleagues of the staff. From beginning to end of the campaign, the Germans showed the same embarrassing skill in appearing where they ought not to have appeared. They did not, in fact, play the game. When we were at Landrecies in the early spring, we set up a semi-permanent fuel park. This great idea, which had originated at G.H.Q., was conceived in terms of the kind of war which never, as things turned out, existed anywhere except on paper. One fine morning in May, the officer in charge ran into a column of tanks in the main street. They were, he thought, painted a very odd colour, but that did not worry him overmuch, because he could not possibly know all the various types in use in the French Army. But what *did* upset him considerably was the very curious route that they seemed to be taking! They were moving in the direction of Cambrai; in other words, *away* from the front. But that, too, could be explained without much difficulty, since it was only natural that in the

47

winding streets of a little town the guides might go wrong. He was just about to run after the commander of the convoy in order to put him right, when a casual passer-by, better informed than he was, shouted—'Look out! they're Germans!'

It can be seen from what I have said that the war was a constant succession of surprises. The effect of this on morale seems to have been very serious. And here I must touch on a delicate subject. I have no right to do more than record impressions which are those only of a looker-on. But there are some things that must be said, even at the risk of hurting a good many feelings. Men are so made that they will face expected dangers in expected places a great deal more easily than the sudden appearance of deadly peril from behind a turn in the road which they have been led to suppose is perfectly safe. Years ago, shortly after the Battle of the Marne, I saw men who the day before had gone into the line under murderous fire without turning a hair, run like rabbits just because three shells fell quite harmlessly on a road where they had piled arms in order to furnish a water-fatigue. 'We cleared out because the Germans came.' Again and again I heard that said in the course of last May and June. Analysed, the words mean no more than this: 'Because the Germans turned up where we didn't expect them and where we had never been told we ought to expect them.' Consequently, certain breakdowns, which cannot, I fear, be denied, occurred mainly because men had been trained to use their brains too slowly. Our soldiers were defeated and, to some extent, let themselves be too easily defeated, principally because their minds functioned far too sluggishly.

Not only did we meet the enemy too often in unexpected places, but for the most part, especially, and with increasing frequency, *in a way* which neither the High Command nor, as a result, the rank and file had anticipated. We should have been perfectly prepared to spend whole days potting at one another from entrenched positions, even if the lines had been only a few yards apart as they were in the Argonne during the last war. It would have seemed to us the most natural thing in the world to carry out raids on occupied saps. It would have been well within our capacity to stand firm in face of an assault through a curtain of wire more or less cut by 'Minenwerfer', or to have gone over the top courageously in an attempt to rush a position that had already been flattened—though, as a rule, not very completely—by artillery fire. In short, we could have played our part without difficulty in operations beautifully planned by our own staff and the enemy's, if only they had been in accordance with the well-digested lessons learned at peace-time manœuvres. It was much more terrifying to find ourselves suddenly at grips with a section of tanks in open country. The Germans took no account of roads. They were everywhere. They felt their way forward, stopping whenever they ran up against serious resistance. Where, however, the resistance was not serious and they could find a 'soft spot', they drove ahead, exploiting their gains, and using them as a basis from which to develop the appropriate tactical movement or, rather, as it seemed, to take their choice of a number of alternative possibilities already envisaged in accordance with that methodical opportunism which was so characteristic of Hitler's methods. They relied on action and on improvisation. We, on the other hand, believed in doing nothing and in behaving as we always had behaved.

Nothing could better illustrate all this than the final episodes of the campaign in which I took a personal part. That was the time at which it really did seem as though we were beginning to profit by the lessons of experience. A decision was taken to group the forces which were in retreat from Normandy and were already cut off by the enemy advance west of Paris from the armies which had fallen back on the Loire, and with them to hold Brittany. Well, what happened? A thoroughly reliable general of engineers was hurriedly sent to reconnoitre a 'position' with both flanks resting on the sea. It was unthinkable to a staff that we should put up any kind of resistance without first plotting on the map and then pegging out on the ground a fine continuous 'line' complete with switches, forward positions, battle zones, and all the rest of it. True, we had neither the time available to organize such a system, guns with which to equip the various strong-points, or ammunition for those guns even supposing that we had found them. The result of all this was that after a few bursts of machine-gun fire, exchanged, I believe, at Fougères, the Germans entered Rennes (which our great defence system had been designed to cover) without fighting, swarmed over the peninsula, and took hordes of prisoners.

Is it true to say that by then—the precise moment at which Pétain announced that he had asked for an armistice—all hope of resistance had become impossible? Several officers thought not, especially the younger officers, for, with the quickened pace of events, a wider gulf began to show between the generations. Unfortunately, our leaders were not drawn from among those who suffered least from a hardening of the arteries. I am still strongly of the opinion to-day that what we called, in 1918, our 'last-ditchers' were right. They dreamed of a modern type of warfare waged by guerrillas against tanks and motorized detachments. Some of them, if I am not wrong, had drawn up plans for such a war, plans which will never now see the light of day. The motorcyclists, of whom the enemy made such extensive and such excellent use, could move rapidly, and without too many accidents, only on metalled roads. Even vehicles equipped with caterpillar treads proceed less slowly on macadamized highways than across open country, and mobile guns and tractors of the normal type must have a good hard surface on which to manœuvre. That is why the Germans, true to their doctrine of speed, tended more and more to move their shock elements along the main arteries. It was, therefore, absolutely unnecessary to cover our front with a line extending for hundreds of kilometres, almost impossible to man, and terribly easy to pierce. On the other hand, the invader might have been badly mauled by a few islands of resistance well sited along the main roads, adequately camouflaged, sufficiently mobile, and armed with a few machine-guns and anti-tank artillery, or even with the humble 75! In Rennes I saw a German column, composed for the most part of motorcyclists, moving unopposed down the Boulevard Sévigné, and all the old instincts of the foot-slogger stirred in me. But I could do nothing, because the only men available were a few orderly-room clerks and storekeepers, who, from the earliest days of the war, had been, quite ridiculously, kept unarmed. I was badly tempted, all the same, to lie in wait for that damned column at the corner of some spinney of the Breton country-side, which is so admirably suited by nature for the mounting of ambushes, even if we had nothing to fight with but the sparse equipment of an engineer detachment. Once we had produced confusion in the enemy ranks, it would have been easy enough for us to melt into the 'wild', and then repeat the same performance farther on. I am quite certain that three-quarters of the men would have jumped at the chance of playing a game like that. But, alas, the regulations had never envisaged such a possibility.

Naturally enough, this high-speed type of warfare demands a certain specialized equipment. The Germans saw to it that such equipment was available: we, on the other hand, did not, or only in insufficient quantities. It has been said, not once but again and again, that we were short of tanks, aeroplanes, guns, motor vehicles, and tractors, and that, consequently, we were never, from the very beginning of hostilities, in a position to fight as we ought to have fought. All this is, unfortunately, true enough, and it is equally true that the causes of this lamentable and fatal policy were not, all of them, wholly military. About that I shall have something to say later. The faults of some do not, however, excuse those of others, and it would be highly unbecoming in the High Command to put in a plea of 'Innocent'.[1]

Let us, if we like, condemn the strategic blunders which compelled our troops in the Nord Department either to abandon to the enemy, or to jettison on the Flanders beaches, the equipment of three motorized divisions, several regiments of mobile artillery, and all the tanks belonging to one of our armies. This material would have come in mighty handy on the battlefields of the Somme or the Aisne, for never had the nation in arms been better 'found'. But I am not for the moment concerned with that. I want, rather, to consider the preparations that were made before war broke out. If we were short of tanks, aeroplanes, and tractors, it was mainly because we had put our not inexhaustible supplies of money and labour into *concrete*. But even so, we had not been wise enough to erect enough of it on our northern frontier, which is just as much open to attack as our eastern. And why? Because we had been taught to put our whole trust in the Maginot Line—constructed at vast expense and with much blowing of trumpets—only to see it turned, and even pierced, on the Rhine for the simple reason that it had been allowed to stop short on our left flank (but about that astonishing incident of the crossing of the Rhine I know only what the newspapers told us, which was precisely nothing at all) because, at the last

---

[1] I am now in a better position than I was to realize that, though our military equipment was undoubtedly insufficient, it was not lacking to the extent that is sometimes supposed. It certainly did not appear at the front in sufficient quantities, but that does not mean that farther back there were not plenty of tanks immobilized in store, and a considerable number of aeroplanes which never took the air. Many of these tanks and aeroplanes had never even been assembled. What, for instance, happened at Villacoublay when the Germans were advancing on Paris? Is it true, as I have heard, that several aeroplanes had to be destroyed on the ground because there were not enough pilots capable of taking them up? The story is by no means improbable. I know one peace-time pilot who, though mobilized, was never, in the whole course of the war, allowed to handle a military machine. (July 1942.)

moment, a hurried decision was taken to construct a number of concrete block-houses in the Department of the Nord, which, since they were designed with only a frontal field of fire, were taken from behind, with the result that our men had to expend all their efforts on digging a magnificent anti-tank ditch covering Cambrai and Saint-Quentin—which the Germans overran one fine day by the simple expedient of advancing against it *from* those two places; because the doctrine then current among our military theorists laid it down that we had reached one of those moments in the history of strategy when the power of defensive armour to resist is greater than the power of gun-fire to pierce—in other words, when the fortified position is practically impregnable—though, unfortunately, the High Command lacked the courage, when the decisive moment came, to remain loyal to a theory which would, at least, have condemned the Belgian adventure even before it had started; because many of our military pundits were profoundly suspicious of armoured units, judging them too heavy to be moved easily (and their rate of progress as shown in official statistics was, it is true, very slow, but only because it was assumed that they *must* move by night—for security reasons—whereas, as things turned out, the war of speed was conducted almost uniformly by day); because those attending the Cavalry courses at the Staff College had had it drilled into them that, though tanks might be tolerably useful in defence, their value for attack was nil; because our technical experts—or those who passed for such—were of the opinion that bombardment by artillery was far superior to bombing from the air, oblivious of the fact that ammunition for guns has to be brought up over great distances, while the rate at which aeroplanes can be replenished is limited only by the speed of their flight; because, to sum up, our leaders, blind to the many contradictions inherent in their attitude, were mainly concerned to renew in 1940 the conditions of the war they had waged in 1914–18.

One of the Vanquished gives Evidence

The Germans, on the contrary, had been thinking in terms of 1940.[1]

The story goes that Hitler, before drawing up his final plans for the campaign, summoned a number of psychologists to his headquarters and asked their advice. I cannot vouch for the truth of this, but it does not seem to be altogether beyond the bounds of probability. However that may be, the air offensive, conducted with such dash by the Germans, does seem to prove that they had gone very deeply into the whole question of nerves and the best way of breaking them. Nobody who has ever heard the whistling scream made by dive-bombers before releasing their load is ever likely to forget the experience. It is not only that the strident din made by the machines terrifies the victim by awakening in his mind associated images of death and destruction. In itself, and by reason of what I may call its strictly acoustic qualities, it can so work upon the nerves that they become wrought to a pitch of intolerable tension whence it is a very short step to panic. There is good evidence that these noises were deliberately intensified by various mechanical means. Aerial bombardment as developed by the Germans is never *primarily* designed as a method of spreading massacre and material desolation. No matter how thickly bombs may be sown, they never, in fact, register hits on more than a relatively small number of men. But the effect of bombing on the nerves is far-reaching, and

[1] The machine is a new-comer. That, I am sure, is why our professional strategists disliked it so much. In a book written by a Frenchman, J. de Pierrefeu (*Plutarch a menti*, p. 300), the following passage occurs: 'Robert de Beauplan, who was sent by the *Matin* to cover the famous *Circuit de l'Est* which revealed to the people of France the marvels of our national aviation, told me of a remarkable conversation which he had had with General Foch (then commanding the Xth Corps) at the close of that highly successful display. As the spectators on the plateau of Malzéville were going back to their cars, Foch took him familiarly by the arm and said: "I won't deny it's a delightful sport, but the value of the aeroplane for army work is practically zero." ' Compare with this the remarkable paper written by Marshal Pétain on the dangers of motorization. But between 1914 and 1918 even the strategists had had time to learn their lesson. (July 1942.)

54

can break the potential of resistance over a large area. It was doubtless with that end in view that the enemy High Command sent wave after wave of bombers to attack us. The result came up only too well to their expectations.

Once again I find myself constrained to deal with a subject on which even to touch—so far, at least, as this war is concerned—gives me an acute feeling of discomfort. Only those who have shared with their comrades the existence of the front line have any right to speak about danger, courage, and the hesitancies that afflict even the brave. I realize that. All the same, I am going to relate one small experience of my own, and without mincing words. I underwent my baptism of fire in 1940 (my earlier baptism of 1914 took place at the Marne) on 22 May on a road in Flanders—for I do not count the bombing of Douai and of the environs of Lens, in neither of which was I closely concerned. On the morning of the day in question, the convoy of which my car formed part was first machine-gunned from the air and then bombed. The machine-gunning, though it killed a man quite close to me, left me more or less unmoved. Of course, it is never very pleasant to be within touching-distance of death, and I do not mind admitting that I was a good deal relieved when the storm of bullets passed. But all through that particular episode my uneasiness had been much more a matter of intellect than of instinct. It was a sort of *cold* fear, with nothing in it of the quality of genuine *terror*. The bombing attack, so far as I am aware, killed no one, or no one who was anywhere near me. Nevertheless, it left me profoundly shaken, and when I crept out of the ditch where I had been crouching I was trembling pretty badly. During the latter part of the campaign I came under a number of artillery bombardments. I have known worse, and should be the last to exaggerate their violence. Still, they were quite nasty enough. But I stood up to them without much difficulty, and I think I can say that they never made me lose my presence of mind. But under air bombing I was never able to retain anything like the same calmness except by making a very considerable effort of will.

It is true, of course, that my reflexes had, to some extent, been conditioned. Ever since my Argonne experiences of 1914 the whine of bullets had become stamped on the grey matter of my brain as on the wax of a gramophone record, so that the mere turning of the handle would start that particular tune playing: nor were my ears so faultily constructed as to have lost, in rather less than a quarter of a century, the art they had learned of guessing the trajectory of a shell and judging its probable point of impact. My experiences of air bombardment had been far less frequent. Faced by that particular danger I was about as green as the youngest recruit among us. Still, the difference in emotional 'temperature' of the three kinds of experience I have been describing was so general to all of us that I am forced to the conclusion that its cause lay deeper than can be accounted for by the nature of my own private reactions. Admittedly, the almost complete absence of our own fighters from the sky above our heads, and the deplorable immunity thus enjoyed by the enemy bombers, played no small part in lowering the morale of the troops. But these things do not wholly explain what happened.

Air bombing is probably, in itself, no more *actually* dangerous than many other kinds of peril to which the soldier is exposed— or not, at any rate, in open country. When men are caught inside houses, the collapse of walls and the atmospheric concussion consequent upon any explosion in a confined space always result in a high death-roll. In the open, on the other hand, artillery fire, even when fairly widely distributed, accounts for at least as many victims, while machine-gunning is without parallel as a method of slaughter, since it literally spares no one. From the moment the campaign opened, we had been struck by the relatively small number of losses attributable to enemy aeroplanes, though the reports of their activity reaching us from the front were very highly coloured.

No, the fact is that this dropping of bombs from the sky has a unique power of spreading terror. They are dropped from a great height, and seem, though quite erroneously, to be falling straight on top of one's head. The combination of weight and altitude gives them an appearance of almost visible violence which no shelter, however thick, seems capable of resisting. There is something inhuman about the nature of the trajectory and the sense of power. Exposed to this unleashing of destruction, the soldier cowers as under some cataclysm of nature, and is tempted to feel that he is utterly defenceless—though, in reality, if one dives into a ditch or even throws oneself flat on the ground, one is pretty safe from the bursts, which are generally a good deal less effective than those of shells, always ruling out, of course, the effects of a direct hit. One has, whether under air or artillery bombardment, what old soldiers call 'pretty good elbow room'. The noise is hateful, savage, and excessively nerve-racking, both that of the descending 'whistle' (deliberately accentuated) about which I have already spoken, and that of the actual burst, which shakes every bone in one's body. It seems to crush the very air with unparalleled violence, and conjures up pictures of torn flesh which are only too horribly borne out in fact by the sights one sees. It is not only that the bodies are terribly mangled. The effect of escaping gases adds to the appalling nature of the spectacle. A man is always scared of dying, but particularly so when to death is added the threat of complete physical disintegration. No doubt this is a peculiarly illogical manifestation of the instinct of self-preservation, but its roots are very deep in human nature. Had the war lasted longer, it is probable that our men would have acquired, in this matter of aerial bombardment, some of the contempt bred of familiarity without which no one can stand up to danger effectively. Reason would have convinced them that, no matter how terrible it might be, its material effects were no worse than those of other forms of attack.

One of the Vanquished gives Evidence

In a war of which speed was the one essential, it was of the first importance that we should be able to gauge our enemy's psychology accurately. But what a roar of laughter there would have been had somebody so much as suggested to the General Staff that it might be well to pay some attention to a few old cranks who happened to be experts in the art of measuring sensations!

To what extent is it justifiable to speak of there having been an absence of 'order' in the various staffs? Quite apart from the fact that habits of work varied from group to group or general to general, one should be very careful indeed about employing such a phrase. There is more than one kind of order, and, therefore, more than one kind of its 'lack'. All the staffs on which I ever worked had, to an almost morbid degree, the passion for 'paper'. Writing had to be very neat. The style of expression had to be in accordance with an inflexible tradition. In the preparation of statistical tables the figures had to be alined as regularly as soldiers on parade. All files had to be carefully docketed, and all incoming and outgoing correspondence properly registered. From such details is built 'order' in the bureaucratic sense. It was only natural that it should flourish among men who had received, in time of peace, what amounted to an intensive bureaucratic training. Far be it from me to despise such things. A properly organized routine compels men to express themselves lucidly and saves a great deal of time. But it is a pity that this admirable concern for cleanliness in paper-work should not always be extended to the *places* in which that work is done. I have never seen a dirtier or more fetid interior than that of a certain headquarters office in the fortified zone. Any company-sergeant-major who had permitted in his barrack-rooms even half the quantity of dust that covered our tables and filled our cupboards would very soon have lost his stripes. True, I have known ante-rooms of ministers, whom no one could have accused of aping the military, which were scarcely more attractive.

But that is no excuse. Some people may think that I am over-stressing trivial details. I have, I admit, a strong dislike of slovenliness. It is infectious, and easily worms its way into the mind. To get rid of it would be an admirable reform, and I commend it to the attention of those who are concerned with putting our national house in order.

There was, however, another side to the praiseworthy paper routine of our military staffs. It led to a waste of energy which might have been much better employed in other directions. Among my fellow reservists were a number of senior civil servants and directors of big private concerns. They were all, like myself, amazed at having to spend their time doing the kind of office work which, in civil life, they would have entrusted to very junior clerks. When I was in charge of fuel supplies at Army H.Q. I had to give every evening over a period of months to entering up the figures of my daily issues. I took as little time over it as possible, and soon grew expert in a species of arith-metical acrobatics, though at first, I confess, I did find that I was a bit out of practice. But once the general lines of our peculiar form of accountancy had been laid down, any clerk could have done the work just as well. Nor was my case exceptional. The question of 'secrecy' did not enter into the matter at all, because my rough drafts were always copied out later by a private soldier. Besides, a few minutes spent in nosing round our offices, which were plastered with maps showing the location of all munition dumps, fuel depots, and rail-heads in the Army area, would have given much precious information to any spy who might have succeeded in passing himself off as one of the clerical staff. The fact of the matter is that the headquarters organizations of the French Army resembled business houses with departmental managers—represented by the officers—at the top, stenographers at the bottom, and, in between, nothing at all. It would have been the simplest thing in the world to recruit a number of highly qualified 'confidential clerks' from N.C.O.s of the reserve.

One of the Vanquished gives Evidence

It is a bad thing for men who have to carry a heavy load of responsibility, who ought to keep their sense of initiative keen, to be constantly kept back by the need of performing purely mechanical tasks. If, too, the staffs had been better supplied with N.C.O.s, it would probably have been possible, at least where the anxieties of the fighting front were not too pressing, to have released a number of officers for more useful employment elsewhere.

But how was it that on many of us, and particularly, I gather, on regimental officers, the staff formation produced an undeniable impression of disorder as soon as the war entered its active phase? The explanation may, I think, be found in the fact that the static order of office routine is, in many respects, the very antithesis of the active and perpetually inventive 'order' which movement demands. One is a matter of discipline and training, the other of imaginative realism, adaptable intelligence, and, above all, of character. The two kinds are not mutually exclusive, but the first does not necessarily imply the second, and often, unless great care is taken, is a bad school for it. All through that long period of waiting which wrought such havoc in our armies, the peace-time habits of neatness and order, of which we were so proud, had the effect of slowing down the tempo of our lives. When we were suddenly called upon to act swiftly, our leaders, more often than not, mistook feverish activity for quick decision.

Keeping a lot of routine papers in order does not call for much mental effort. Quite a different sort of self-mastery is required when it becomes a question of drawing up, well in advance and with the maximum of elasticity, plans which may have to wait a long time before they are put in action, and may, at the last moment, have to be adapted to the needs of a chaotic situation. My first experience of the machinery of mobilization in 1939 gave me a bad headache. I will not discuss here the system of depots which was substituted after the last war for the old corps organizations. I know that the scheme met with a good deal of hostile criticism, some of it at a high level. It seemed to me bound, by its very nature, to produce delays and difficulties. Most of the clothing and equipment was still being supplied by the various corps, and in order to get all this material to the Intake Depots, a whole system of transport, unsuitable in form and necessarily slow in movement, had to be organized. Nobody seemed to have realized that the fitting out of reservists of forty with uniforms made for young conscripts, or the handling of heavy requisitioned draught-horses with the discarded harness of a cavalry stable, meant saddling the wretched depots, whether 'main' or 'secondary', with problems which were, in themselves, quite incapable of solution. The work, too, involved much niggling detail, and, quite often, was entrusted to the wrong type of person. I do not mean to say that I have not come across several highly competent depot commanders: I have. But I have also had experience of a great many who were far from competent—captains and colonels due for pension, who had all the faults commonly attributed to the regular N.C.O. Once the new system had been adopted it should, in view of the difficulties that were bound to arise, have been operated by carefully selected men, and should have ranked high in the list of 'seniorities' when promotion came to be considered. Army circles always find it difficult to realize that the 'showiness' of a job has nothing whatever to do with its importance, or that those engaged in what seem to be very humble tasks are often just as deserving of recognition as their more fortunate fellows.

But whether the system of Recruit Depots was good or bad—and I have no doubt that it has many advantages—it cannot excuse the mistakes that occurred, which had nothing to do with the general principle. No officer, I think, who was called upon to do duty with one of these regional organizations, or with a Subdivisional Area Group, will ever remember without a wry smile the incredible tangle of 'measures', all duly numbered, which were supposed to be taken during the so-called 'Alert

Period' preceding actual mobilization. Dragged from one's bed in the middle of the night by a telegram which might read, for instance, 'Measure 81 to come into force immediately', one would rush to the code-card which was always kept handy, only to find that 'Measure 81' involved the implementation of all clauses contained in 'Measure 49' with the exception of such of them as might have been already set in motion by the application of 'Measure 93'—should the latter happen to have come into force earlier than its numerical place in the series seemed to warrant, and that, in any case, the two first paragraphs of 'Measure 57' must also be acted upon. I pick on these numbers at random, and am not prepared, at this distance of time, to say that they are accurate. Those with whom I worked will, I think, agree that I have shown the whole business as being a good deal simpler than it actually was. Can one wonder that in such circumstances mistakes were of frequent occurrence? For instance, as a result of not reading instructions with sufficient care, the police authorities of Alsace-Lorraine proceeded, in September 1939, to carry out a premature massacre of all the carrier-pigeons of three departments. I do not say that the officers sitting far away in Paris, in a dark little office of the rue Saint-Dominique, adding figure to figure until the result was like a Chinese puzzle, were necessarily lacking in imagination. It was only that their particular type of imagination was not calculated to give them a clear idea of what it would mean to carry out their orders.

But that was far from being the worst of many errors. I know of one depot in Strasbourg, situated close to the river-bank, which was well within range of the enemy's light artillery, and even of his machine-guns. Another had been established in one of the neighbouring forts which was also within easy reach of the Rhine. It could be approached only by one bridge laid across the defensive ditch. A single well-placed bomb or shell would have turned the place into a death-trap. Nothing of the kind, I shall be told, did in fact happen. Agreed. But how could we be sure beforehand that the Germans would not fire on Strasbourg? The truth of the matter is that this particular arrangement was perfectly all right so long as the bridgehead at Kehl was a demilitarized area. Unfortunately, when it ceased to be so, the High Command forgot to modify its arrangements, or did not modify them sufficiently.

I must say something too about the appalling confusion which marked the one piece of mobilization of which I had personal experience. It concerned the calling-up of certain territorial elements which came for orders under a Subdivisional Area Group. When our general took over his command we discovered with horrified amazement that there was no list of the units of which it was to be composed. We had to improvise one as best we could—and it was a poor best—by dint of hunting our way through a chaotic mass of files. As a result, the most frightful confusion reigned within each unit, and they were all mixed up anyhow. In one part of our zone we had two sections under command of an officer who belonged to a totally different group, and in another several companies but no colonel. Our splendid lines-of-communication troops consisted of elderly men whose willingness was equalled only by their ingenuity in making the best of a bad job. Very few of them had a sound pair of boots, but none of them, by the grace of God, actually died of hunger. How one section which I spent a whole day trying to find on the main line to Saint-Dié managed to live at all, I shall never know. It is not fair, I admit, to argue from the particular to the general. I have good reason to believe that the mobilization in our little corner of France had not been very well planned. The senior officer in charge had little to show for his staff training but a certain easy-going irresponsibility, and most of the work was actually done by his juniors. This, admittedly, was only a solitary instance, but it gave cause for grave disquiet. By 1940 we realized that a good many mistakes had been put right, but not all of them by any means. The depots had not been moved, and the lines-of-communication troops still tramped the permanent way in sandals or light walking shoes, unless they happened to have furnished themselves with stouter footwear.

One did not need to be possessed of extraordinary gifts of observation at First Army H.Q. to realize, during the months preceding May 1940, that a number of alarming cracks had developed in the military fabric. They were not, in themselves, very dangerous, but it was easy to see that, should a crisis suddenly develop, they might split wide open and let in the flood. One of them was the wholly inadequate organization of our communications.

I have no personal grouse in this matter. Throughout the campaign I was able, without difficulty, to communicate with the various sections of my Fuel-Supply group, and always managed to work smoothly enough with the different units for whose needs I had to cater. Lachamp's intelligent unselfishness was of the greatest possible assistance to me. Naturally, I was careful, wherever possible, not to trespass on his prerogatives as my senior officer. In fact, he exercised them with such competence and authority that I was never once tempted to call his decisions in question. It was agreed between us that, since I was closer to the fountain-head of information than he was, I must always, in cases of real urgency, pass on Army Orders directly to subordinate formations. This system of by-passing saved us, on more than one occasion, a great deal of t:me.[1] We were both of us obsessed, as a result of our experiences during the former

---

[1] My by-passing became pretty extensive. Officially, the Fuel Park was in touch with the Army Commander only through the General Commanding Army Artillery, who was himself represented at a lower level by a Director of Munitions and Fuel. Had we strictly observed the rules of the hierarchy, it would have meant that every order from army to park would have had to go through both these senior authorities. In the matter of official documents this system had always been observed at Bohain, and the consequent delays caused both me and Lachamp many a headache when we thought what might happen under more active conditions. Luckily, when the time came, we were able to do a bit of short-circuiting, and, thanks to the goodwill of the officers concerned, no sparks flew.

war, by blind terror of the frightful games of blind-man's-buff which inevitably occur where systems of communication are inadequately organized. No matter how constant the moves forced upon H.Q. and the Supply Park, we always knew where to find both. Though nothing was ever put down on paper, we managed, between us, to develop an internal system by which we could always be sure of passing on urgent instructions.

I always had in my office two motor-cyclists—one supplied by each of the companies of the mobile supply column. Both of them knew, well in advance of any movement, where their companies would be located, and where they could find the senior supply officer. In addition, one of Lachamp's own officers was permanently attached to me. Four other supply officers served as links with the corps. Each of them, regularly once a day and sometimes oftener, visited both Army H.Q. and the corps to which he himself belonged. These grand chaps, some of them not by any means in their first youth, had a pretty hard time of it travelling roads that were often far from safe. One of them, at the time of our first withdrawal after the advance into Belgium, spent more than twenty-four hours trying to find his Corps H.Q. They could always be relied upon to arrive sooner or later at the point they were making for, and we found them extraordinarily useful. Never once between 11 and 31 May, when it was a question of sending orders or receiving requests for supplies, did I have to use the official channels through which the staff was supposed to communicate with subordinate units. Subsequent events proved beyond question that both orders and requests had reached their destination. Never once, so far as I know, did the fighting troops run short of petrol which our 'Mickeys' (this was the Army nickname for the mobile tanks with their gay little distinguishing mark of a Mickey Mouse) so heroically delivered, often over considerable distances. Nor did we ever abandon to the enemy any of our depots in a fit state to operate. The whole line of our retreat from Mons to Lille was lit by more fires than can ever have been kindled by Attila. Lachamp and his officers saw to it that can after can went into the flames till the last drop was consumed. The only exception to this general rule was the fuel depot at Saint-Quentin. So rapidly and so completely did we lose touch with it that I do not know, to this day, what happened there. Our seniors, realizing by experience that all was going well, soon decided to give us a free hand—for which consideration on their part I am duly grateful.

But I am very much afraid that where this sort of self-government and mutual understanding did not exist, contacts between units and their senior formations, or, on the same level, between one unit and another, left a good deal to be desired. I have more than once heard regimental officers complain that they were left too long without orders, and it is very certain—as I have already shown by citing notorious examples—that the staff was imperfectly informed about what was happening on their section of the front. When roads are crowded, as ours soon became, particularly by refugees, the motor-cycle is the only vehicle that can make any progress at all. I think I am right in saying that Army Signals did not have a single one of these machines. Even the number of cars available was insufficient, and what there were were badly allotted. Not a few of us had been profoundly disturbed, ever since the winter, by this state of affairs which arose from faulty organization and control. But no one bothered to set it to rights, and the evil effects became only too apparent in the course of the campaign.

It must be remembered that, almost as soon as active operations began, Army H.Q. moved from Bohain to Valenciennes so as to reduce the distance separating it from the troops moving into Belgium. As soon as I arrived at Valenciennes in the early afternoon of the 11th, I arranged to go straight on to Mons in order to consult with local Belgian H.Q. about the requisitioning of fuel supplies. It can scarcely be denied that the matter

66

was one of supreme urgency. I discovered that, owing to the fact that all available transport had been formed into a shuttle-service between old and new H.Q. for the purposes of the move, it would be quite impossible for me to proceed. What was the use of my having left Bohain if I could not get forward? Luckily, I was visited during the day by a friendly lawyer of Lille who was acting as adjutant to the commander of a supply group. He had come to beg me for some petrol. With some degree of cynicism I replied: 'Nothing for nothing: no petrol unless you get me a car!' The bargain was struck, and I set off for Mons at last. The lesson was a salutary one, and I immediately set about arranging my own system of communications along the lines I have already described.

It would have been a miracle indeed if orders *had* reached their intended recipients in time, seeing that only too often Army had no idea where its corps were situated. On one occasion, when the Cavalry Corps had done a move, the supply liaison officer set off, as usual, to make contact with those privileged customers. When he got back I took him along to Intelligence, thinking it as well to make sure that our great tacticians really did know where the new H.Q. was to be found. It then appeared that there was a difference amounting to thirty kilometres between the actual spot and the one they had pencilled in on their maps. I can still hear the very grudging 'thanks' which was the reward for our intervention. Some time later I wanted Lachamp to go to British H.Q. The occasion was an important one, having no less an object than to arrange for the destruction of the Lille dumps. But where on earth *was* Lord Gort's H.Q.? Crossing once again the awe-inspiring threshold of Intelligence, I asked. B . . . replied, without batting an eyelid, that they had no idea. I was fortunate enough to be able to lay my hands on a chit that was going the rounds in which that piece of information, along with others of a like nature, was contained. Our friends were less ill informed than they thought! But the fact that the officer in charge of operations could tolerate for a single moment the idea of being deprived, for want of an elementary piece of topo-graphical information, of all means of communicating with the headquarters of Allied troops supposed to be working on our left flank, and could calmly admit to an ignorance which he was, in fact, in a position to dissipate, throws an ugly light on our methods of work.

And now that I have touched on the subject of 'The English', I feel bound to ask whether we ever really got our co-operation with them properly organized. Never was the fatal insufficiency of our 'liaison', in the fullest sense of that term, more crudely shown up.

But the whole problem of an alliance that turned out so ill is too complicated, and has already given rise to too much heated and ill-natured argument, to be touched on in a mere aside. It is time that somebody had the courage, once and for all, to come to grips with it. This I intend to do, so far, that is, as my experience fits me for the task.

I have many good friends in Great Britain. They have been the soul of hospitality, and have smoothed the way for me in my attempts to understand a civilization for which I have long felt a deep sympathy. To-day they are nearer than ever to my heart, for they, and their fellow countrymen, are shouldering, unaided and at imminent peril of their lives, the task of defend-ing a cause for which I would gladly have died. Whether or not they will ever see what I am about to write, I cannot tell. If they do, they may well feel genuinely shocked. But lack of sincerity is not one of their national faults, and I can only hope that they will forgive my frankness.

The anglophobia of many thousands of Frenchmen is to-day being exploited in the most despicable fashion. It is no manner of use to deny its existence. Its causes are many and various. Some are linked with historical memories which are tougher than a good many people seem to think. The ghost of the 'Maid', the hateful figures of Pitt and Palmerston, have never altogether ceased to haunt a collective mind which is only too ready to remember the past. It might be a good thing if an old-established nation could forget more easily, because memory often distorts the image of the present, and the crying need of most men is that they should be able to adapt themselves to new conditions. There are other causes, too, which are more artificial and a great deal more blameworthy. The regular readers of a certain weekly, much enjoyed in Army circles, were told at the time of the Italian invasion of Ethiopia that it was our duty to ensure the 'destruction' of England. The article was signed with what, to all appearances, was a French name. But who were its real instigators? We all know that they were no countrymen of ours. But there is more to it than that.

It must, I think, be regarded as inevitable that two nations, so different as ours are—different in spite of having in common many of their most fundamental ideas—should find it very difficult to know, to understand, and, consequently, to love one another. This truth holds good on either side of the Channel, and I do not suppose that among average English people, especially of the lower middle class, the age-old prejudices against the 'Frenchies' opposite have even now ceased to flourish. Ours certainly have not. But it is not to be denied that certain episodes in the course of our recent, and all too short, fellowship in arms were not calculated to thin the fog of misunderstanding.

The conscripted element counted for very little in the British forces which, during those long months of waiting, settled down with us on the plains of Flanders, lived in our villages, and policed our roads. Most of the men and officers were 'regulars', and they had, I am sure, all the excellences that one associates with professional soldiers—as well as some of their faults. The soldier immortalized by Kipling knows how to obey and how to fight. Once again he was to show his mettle when asked to shed his blood on the battlefields of Belgium. But he is, by nature, a looter and a lecher: that is to say, he is guilty of two vices which the French peasant finds it hard to forgive when both are satisfied to the detriment of his farmyard and his daughters. Nor does the Englishman show to his best advantage when he is on the Continent—unless, that is, he belongs to the more educated classes. In his own country he is, as a rule, kindly and good-natured, but once across the Channel he tends to confuse his European hosts with 'natives'—in other words, with those inhabitants of his colonial possessions who are, by definition, his 'inferiors'. His natural shyness serves but to intensify his unfriendliness. These, I admit, are trivial matters when compared with the deep, underlying currents of feeling concerned with great national issues. No one, however, will, I think, deny that they weigh heavily in the scales with country people like ours who make a point of being suspicious of all foreigners and live within the close limits of their selfish interests.

Then, after long and terrible weeks, came the moment of embarkation. I am not one of those who bitterly resent the fact that the British should have insisted on having priority in this matter, or should have refused, with very few exceptions, to let our men on to the ships before they had got the full complement of their own troops away from the beaches. Save for those of our men who were engaged in coastal defence, their own army was the nearest to the sea, and, naturally, they were not prepared to see their own personnel and material swallowed up in a disaster for which they did not hold themselves responsible. When the British 'Tars' had seen their own countrymen to safety, they turned their attention to ours. The spirit of self-sacrifice which they showed in the face of danger, and their kindliness, was no less when exercised on our behalf than it had been when they were dealing with their first consignment of passengers.

But here again it is essential that we try to understand the

Frenchman's inevitable reactions. Our men, deprived by their own leaders of the power to resist, had been desperately waiting on the long Flanders beaches, or among the dunes, for their last chance of escaping capture by the enemy, and long months of incarceration in the prisons of the Third Reich. With each day that passed they felt the Germans creeping closer, and each day were exposed to a growing violence of bombing. They knew well enough that not all of them would succeed in getting away, nor, in fact, did they. In such circumstances they would have needed a superhuman dose of charity not to feel bitter as they saw ship after ship drawing away from the shore, carrying their foreign companions in arms to safety. Heroes they may have been, but they were not saints. Add to all this a number of irritating incidents which, though difficult to prevent in the state of nervous tension then existing, were bound to have a bad effect on men already suffering from intolerable strain. There was, for instance, the case—and I can vouch that it did really occur—of the French interpreter with an English brigade, who, after long months of intimate companionship in billets and on the battle-field, found himself left to his own devices on the sands, and forbidden to set foot on the ship which he saw steaming away with his former friends lining the rails. The touching kindness with which a great number of our men found themselves welcomed once they got across to England did much to heal these wounds. But it was not always in evidence. The welcome of the man in the street was invariably warm and affectionate; that of the authorities, on the other hand, was too often cold and needlessly suspicious. Certain transit camps had an almost penal air. Harassed troops are always difficult to handle. It is not to be wondered at that officials who were called upon to deal with a situation of considerable delicacy, and were obsessed by the need to keep discipline, should now and then have been guilty of clumsiness. But it is natural, too, that when such incidents occurred, they should leave lasting traces in men's memories.

One of the Vanquished gives Evidence

It has often been said that the British gave us insufficient assistance. This charge was made with the object of covering up our own failure, with the result that a good many of the figures quoted in its support were cooked. I have very good reason to know that the British had many more than three divisions in Flanders. Still, this pernicious propaganda did not have to rely altogether on falsifications.

Those who have some knowledge of the political and social traditions of the English—which are so different from ours—realize that their adoption of the conscript method of enlistment was an act of great courage. It is difficult, however, to deny that this act of courage came rather late in the day, nor is it altogether surprising that Frenchmen between the ages of thirty and forty, finding themselves under fire, should sometimes have wondered why it was that their English contemporaries were allowed to remain safely at home. Great Britain has, since then, made up only too well in sacrifice for her tardiness in preparation. But who, at the time of the retreat, was in a position to see into the future? It is, too, beyond question that when our First Army was planning to launch a break-through offensive from the north, southwards towards Arras, in conjunction with French troops operating in the reverse direction from the Somme, British H.Q. countermanded, almost at the last moment, the assistance which it had already promised. This decision, as was but natural, sowed a plentiful harvest of resentment, nor was there any lack of those ready to exploit it. I am reminded, in this connexion, of something that happened a little later, at the time of the Belgian capitulation. When the news reached us, an Intelligence officer was heard to remark, sceptically, '*What* a chance for General Blanchard!' We had, in fact, been surrounded for some considerable time before Leopold III surrendered, and the enemy encirclement was already half-way to completion when the British threw a spanner into the wheels of the projected offensive. What better excuse for our own failures than the mistakes of others?

72

We of the Northern Army had, finally, to give up any hope of breaking into the 'German pocket'. The British refusal had certainly contributed to the collapse of that enterprise even before it developed. The form in which it came, however, was not very courteous. If, taking things at their worst, a sudden deterioration in the strategic situation had, in fact, made it impossible to give effect to the plan already decided upon, it would have been better if British Expeditionary Force G.H.Q. had not left the French High Command quite so long in a state of uncertainty. (But in this matter I have, naturally, heard only one side of the case—our own.) The British decision was probably a sound one.[1] In any case, the historian, whose business it is to understand and not to judge, can explain it without much difficulty. At this point it becomes necessary to take a look at the other side of the medal.

It took a long time to mount our own offensive towards the south. Preliminary reconnaissance, the assembly of the assault troops, the artillery preparation, in short, all the steps regarded as indispensable by current military theory, demanded a great deal of time. Zero hour had already been put back once. The operation envisaged was to have been a Battle of Malmaison in miniature. Whether the pace could have been quickened I do not know: probably not when the Army was holding a line that extended as far as the Escaut. What, however, I do know is that to move in this leisurely fashion meant running the risk of being anticipated by the enemy. By behaving as we did, we gave him every opportunity to strengthen what at first had been merely an advance-guard in the country between our Northern and Southern Armies, and, at the same time, to increase his pressure on the other fronts. Probably our allies, who, meanwhile, had been

---

[1] I have become more and more convinced that it was the only wise decision that could have been taken. What would have been the future of the war if the whole British Army had been pounded to pieces on the continent of Europe in May and June 1940? Still, it was harsh, and it was asking a good deal of the French soldier at the time to see things from so lofty a standpoint.

violently attacked, saw the danger. They disengaged their troops so as not to be involved in the tactical disaster which they foresaw. They had fewer scruples in doing this because they were beginning to feel very impatient at our methods. This failure of confidence is, I think, the psychological explanation of their whole behaviour during the final fortnight of the campaign of Flanders. In the course of a few days we saw the thermometer of the alliance register a heavy fall. It is a matter of general knowledge that the British, from the very outset of hostilities, had accepted the principle of the single command, though admittedly the form it took was by no means complete, and involved many curious consequences. British G.H.Q. came under the orders of our Commander-in-Chief, but only directly. The result of this was that the general commanding our First Army Group, who was in charge of operations from the Ardennes to the sea, found that a not-inconsiderable body of troops over which he exercised no authority had been sandwiched in between the effectives for which he was responsible. At the same time, it must not be forgotten that the concession made by the London Government had had an irritating effect on British national pride, and, in particular, on the minds of the military which are particularly susceptible to offence. The decision was, no doubt, justified by the numerical preponderance of our land forces, which was overwhelming, though the prestige attaching to our military reputation for strategic brilliance had not a little to do with it. Foch, after the Conference of Doullens, had led the Allied armies to victory: it was to be expected that his successor would do the same. Certainly, French officers as a whole were convinced that our staff training was the best in the world, and I have a feeling that they may have been a little too vocal about it.[1] What happened

[1] In the Minutes of the War Council held on 26 April 1940 (*Secret Documents of the French General Staff*, p. 98) there occurs a phrase which well illustrates the intolerable vanity of our senior officers. It was uttered by General Gamelin, and runs as follows: 'It is up to the British to find the bulk of the troops (in Norway). . . . But it is *for us to give them moral support, to organise the strategy of*

was that, in the course of a few days, the entirely unexpected collapse of our armies on the Meuse suddenly threatened all the elements farther to the north with encirclement. Faced by a disaster which might well have involved the loss of the whole of their Expeditionary Force, the British felt that they had a right to be consulted. Their faith in us had already been shaken. The slowness and ineffectiveness of our movements did the rest. Our prestige was a thing of the past, and our Allies made no bones about not concealing the fact. Can one blame them?

When the projected Allied attack on Arras came to nothing, it seems that the two General Staffs, under the influence of mutual disenchantment, gave up almost entirely any further pretence of collaboration. Numerous must have been the bridges (though how numerous I do not know) which the British blew up to cover their retreat, without bothering to find out whether, by their action, they might not be cutting ours. Certainly, in spite of the protests of the engineer-in-charge, they prematurely destroyed the Lille telephone system, thereby depriving the First Army of practically all its means of intercommunication. We considered that they were acting without the slightest consideration for us, and I have no doubt that the very natural disappointment they felt at the failure of our High Command did lead some of them to forget at times what was owing to fighting soldiers whose courage had never been called in question.

A clearer demarcation of the zones for which each army was responsible would probably have prevented a number of tiresome incidents from ever having developed at all. But there was no longer any authority capable of carrying through such a scheme. Up till then areas had been allotted by French G.H.Q. Some sort of friendly arrangement might have been possible. Whether it was ever attempted I cannot say. If it was, it had no success. Lille was a particularly sore point. Nobody knew under

the campaign, and to supply the necessary planning and inspiration. . . .' Alas!
(July 1942.)

whose authority it came. Until 10 May it had certainly been within the British zone; but it was there that the French First Army had carried out its final concentration. For some days it was the main source of our fuel supplies. When it became a question of immobilizing the dumps, we were quite determined not to leave the matter in the hands of our Allies. Their methods seemed to us to be entirely inadequate. They appeared to think that it was enough to put sugar or tar into the petrol. We preferred to burn it. When the problem was laid before General Prioux, he sent a letter and issued an order. The letter, which was addressed to Lord Gort, was interpreted as leaving the decision, in the politest possible way, to the latter. The order, on the contrary, which was circulated to personnel of the First Army assumed that the responsibility would be ours. This manner of solving the problem may have been diplomatically very subtle, but it threw a harsh light on the prevailing uncertainty in regard to the rights of the two armies. The state of confusion continued up to the very last moment. Only one dump escaped being fired. It was situated on the far bank of the canal. The British had already destroyed the bridges and, for some reason unknown to me, refused to allow anybody to cross by boat. Who was responsible for all this chaos? To some extent, probably, the British, though our excessive readiness to accept the situation makes it impossible for us to plead not guilty.

But I am convinced that the breakdown of morale would have been far less total, and would have had consequences a great deal less grave, had our contact with our Allies been, in the first place, more firmly established. Admittedly, it was all very complicated. Lord Gort's Staff performed a double function, acting both as G.H.Q. British Expeditionary Force and as the H.Q. of an Army. As the first of these it was in direct contact with our own Commander-in-Chief, who maintained a French Mission at Lord Gort's H.Q. under the command of General Voruz, who was present as his representative. As the second it was, or should have been, in constant and close touch with the Seventh Army on its left in the coastal area and with the First on its right. Here the French Mission had no standing at all, and it was up to the armies themselves to see that contact did not break down. What happened was that, during the period of waiting, dealings between them were reduced, for the most part, to unimportant questions relating to zone limitation. But it should have been perfectly obvious that, once active operations began, far more urgent problems would come up for settlement, and that their success-ful solution would depend very largely on the means taken earlier to establish mutual collaboration and the sharing of all relevant information. Things turned out, in fact, far worse than anyone had anticipated, because French G.H.Q. having vanished entirely from our field of vision as a result of the German movement of encirclement, the only practical system of communication between the British and ourselves was at Army level.

It will be remembered that I had originally been appointed to act as liaison officer with the British. During our first weeks at Bohain I did my best to carry out my duties in that capacity. No one interfered with me, though no one did much to help me. Later, when I had been put in charge of fuel supplies, I still continued my efforts to establish a workable basis of mutual understanding. On my visits to the British—whose G.H.Q. was at that time dispersed, for reasons of security, in a number of wretched villages round Arras—I found myself having most to do with 'Q Branch'.[1] In addition to my dealings with the fountain-head, I hunted up a Corps H.Q. at Douai, and was also in touch with the French Mission. It soon became clear to me that, though these intermittent contacts might be adequate for the straightening out of minor tangles, they were hopeless so far as any genuine collaboration was concerned.

There can be no real co-operation without comradeship, and comradeship can be achieved only where there is some degree of

[1] 'Q' is an abbreviation for Quartermaster-General's Branch. (*Translator.*)

daily contact. That holds true of all dealings between men, no matter what their nationalities. It is more than ever essential when one is dealing with the British, who are affable, confiding, and even frank, once they have accepted you as a familiar, though deliberately guarded and distant, in spite of their good manners, when they have to do business with somebody who is only an occasional visitor. If you went to see them officially, they would give you perfectly correct answers to any questions you might ask, but nothing more. Probably we should have done just the same. But was that enough? The goal of our endeavours should have been to learn how to handle a war machine which was very different to our own, but with which it had got to be synchronized. It was essential that we should realize what were its weaknesses— if it had any (and what army has not?); that we should under- stand—in order to make others understand later—points of view which did not always, unfortunately, coincide with those of our own High Command; that we should make (and this was the most important point of all) close human contacts, because only when such exist is it possible for either side to offer fruitful sug- gestions without wounding the self-esteem of the other, or to avoid, in the moment of danger, the fatal temptation of putting one's own interest first. All this could never be achieved by occasional visits. We ought to have got into the habit of taking tea together every afternoon, as well as stray whiskies and sodas; we ought to have immersed ourselves in that club atmosphere which is not confined to the mess but serves as a unifying element even when its members are back at their desks. What, in a word, was needed was that we should have an officer of First Army permanently attached to British G.H.Q. This opinion of mine was shared by the Chief of Staff of the French Mission, though his championship remained, unfortunately, without effect owing to the turn taken by events. For that particular Army, less its XVIth Corps, which was detached for the defence of Dunkirk, received orders just after 15 or 16 May (I think) to withdraw altogether from the Antwerp front. Later it was thrown into the breach between the Meuse and the Oise, where it was almost completely wiped out.

Our efforts at First Army were confined to getting permission for an officer from British G.H.Q. to be attached to Intelligence. The first to come was a retired regular who had subsequently gone into the City. His manners, which were at once brusque and hearty, the air he had of enjoying life, and his humour—which, no doubt, seemed more original to us than it would have done to his compatriots—made him popular. He was an enthusiastic soldier, and had the reputation of being very touchy on all matters affecting his authority as representative of the British C.-in-C. It may well be that the rather intemperate zeal of some of my comrades made him suspicious of an interference which he was determined not to brook. My own relations with him were always of the friendliest, but he certainly wanted to keep all the strings in his own hands, and I am afraid that his influence on our senior officers was not always without danger. He was, above all, extremely shrewd, and, in addition, deeply imbued with that social snobbery from which the members of the English upper middle class are rarely free. Nor was he wholly innocent of those national prejudices which are inherent in the old crusted Tory tradition, though he was far too polite to display them.

Only a very simple soul would have expected him to inform us about the weak points in the equipment and methods of our British allies. He left us shortly before 10 May to take up an appointment in the Ministry of Economic Warfare in London. He never, therefore, had an opportunity of rendering those services to the common cause which, I am sure, would have been forthcoming under the stress of danger. With his successor I had very little to do. He was just as delightful, though not so good a mixer. I only once had professional dealings with him, at Lens, when I found him rather over-anxious to shift responsibility.

79

But whatever might be the personal idiosyncrasies of these delegates from an Allied army, even the best of them, when one comes to think of it, could have done no more than supply half the diplomatic representation needed. What Government wishing to maintain contact with a friendly country, to be informed of what is going on, and to establish a solid basis of mutual understanding which may serve as the foundation for a lasting friendship, will ever rest content with offering hospitality to its neighbour's ambassador, and will, on the ground that he is wholly admirable, refuse to send a representative of its own in return?

With this thought in mind, therefore, I took my courage in two hands and asked for an interview with our Chief of Staff, who was then in temporary command of the Army. I put all the arguments to him as best I could, and made it quite plain that I was not after the job of liaison officer at Lord Gort's H.Q. Any such appointment, I said, should be given to somebody far better versed in military theory than I was. But I played my cards badly. Fearful lest my personal opinion might carry too little weight, I supported my case by quoting the more-informed opinion of the head of the French Mission. Alas! It so happened that the lieutenant-colonel to whom I was putting my case was the bosom enemy of that other lieutenant-colonel whose views I was mentioning in support of my own. This ill-fated choice of a guarantor did not help me. The roads of the Staff College are rich in traps for the unwary feet of those who have not been brought up in 'court circles'! I was politely allowed to have my say. My interlocutor made it quite plain that he found my arguments inconclusive, and that, in his opinion, the presence of a British officer at First Army H.Q. was all that was necessary. Later on I did what I could to get the question taken up at French G.H.Q., but again without result. The end of it all was that I grew sick of taking the trouble to travel the Arras road for no better purpose than to indulge in a few minutes of casual conversation, and gave up the whole business. My superiors seemed quite unperturbed by this failure of mine to carry out instructions, and from then on I gave the whole of my time to supervising petrol supplies.

During active operations, one of our senior staff officers, who had already had dealings with the British, acted as our go-between. He was intelligent, and his outlook was a good deal less limited than that of most of his colleagues. I am convinced, not only that he did his best, but that his best was considerably better than what anybody else could have done. But he had never shared the daily life of our Allies, and did not do so even after he had taken up his post, but spent most of his time running from H.Q. to H.Q. The chief trouble was that events were making any real mutual confidence between the two armies less and less easy. Co-operation could have been proof against the difficulties of the time only if it had been firmly based earlier. A genuine alliance is something that has to be worked at all the time. It is not enough to have it set down on paper. It must draw the breath of life from a multiplicity of daily contacts which, taken together, knit the two parties solidly into a single whole. That truth had been too long forgotten at First Army H.Q., and we suffered terribly as a result of our negligence.[1]

As already explained, I spent some time when I first went to First Army, with Intelligence. Later on, my efforts to get a reliable and up-to-date list of Belgian fuel dumps brought me in contact with both Army Group and G.H.Q. Intelligence. I should be a poor historian, indeed, if I had not always taken a particular interest in information and evidence. But just because I was an historian, the methods which I found in use soon filled me with alarm and despondency.

[1] In this matter of the breakdown of liaison between our troops and the British Expeditionary Force, see what Churchill said at the Franco-British War Council of 22 May, and his telegram of the 24th (*Secret Documents of the French General Staff*, pp. 57 and 132). (July 1942.)

One of the Vanquished gives Evidence

Let me make my meaning quite clear. I have no wish to include under a general blanket condemnation a group of men which included a great many who, whether regulars or reservists, were undoubtedly hard-working and competent officers. In the course of my inquiries I was always made welcome at, if not greatly helped by, G.H.Q. Intelligence, and at Army Group I found a degree of understanding, and a willingness to assist, which I valued enormously. At Army things were not so good, and when we were in the mood to talk freely, we made no bones about admitting it. The officer with the charming manners who was in charge of Army Intelligence would have shown to fine advantage at the head of a 'spit and polish' battalion on parade, nor have I any reason to assume that he would not have behaved impeccably on the field of battle. But it was quite clear that he was not up to the job he had been given. Still, the fact that his direction of the work of his office was incompetent cast but the lightest of shadows on our spirits. I had a number of admirable colleagues—I might almost call them friends—on the Intelligence Staff, especially in the interpreters' section, which was in charge of a seasoned old ruffian—in private life he was a little business-man—who rode his subordinates with a light rein. They slaved away, giving of their best, and showed a fine spirit of self-sacrifice not wholly unmixed with shrewdness, in a sphere which was, inevitably, somewhat limited. But it is no good hiding the fact that we were kept very badly supplied with information. I was in a position to see a good deal of the Intelligence work that went on in regard to Belgium. I have already explained that, from the very beginning, G.H.Q. had doled out to us very vague and often erroneous particulars about the position, the capacity, and the contents of the various dumps. Worse still, no steps were taken to see that the mistakes were corrected. We had no idea how the fuel-supply service in the Belgian Army was organized, though, if it came to common action against an aggressor, we should have to work in close collaboration with it.

I did my best to find out. General Blanchard was good enough to sign a personal letter asking for the required details. It remained unanswered. I have reason to suppose that this state of ignorance was not confined to my branch of the service.

It was due to a number of reasons. In the first place, too many people were concerned in the business of gathering information, and there was an ugly atmosphere of competition among them. About this I shall have more to say later. The various military attachés were responsible, not to G.H.Q. but to the War Office, which was always very sensitive where its prerogatives were involved. Under the pretext of a wholly fallacious respect for the needs of neutrality, the War Office and G.H.Q. were in complete agreement on one point—that subordinate formations must, under no conditions, initiate any sort of survey on the other side of the Belgian frontier. As a matter of fact, neither Army nor Group hesitated to do so on their own, and more than one piece of useful information reached us in this more or less clandestine way. Would it not have been far better to have organized these various efforts into a whole?

Improved organization and a keener sense of fact would have been a great advantage. An Intelligence Service ought to act as a kind of agency operating in the interests of the various formations which are—in effect—its customers. It should be in a position to answer questions addressed to it by gunners, air-arm, tanks, and the departments in charge of rail and road movement, as well as by 'G' branch which forms the head of the staff pyramid. Each of these different bodies has demands to make relative to its own peculiar requirements, and these are apt to be neglected by non-specialists. It should be the business of Intelligence to anticipate their needs, and to provide the required facts even before they are demanded. It should circulate to each all relevant information as soon as it is available. But instead of this being done, Intelligence scarcely ever moved outside the narrow limits prescribed for it by a tradition that knew nothing of the needs

83

of mechanical warfare. Its chief preoccupation was the more or less hypothetical establishment of the 'enemy order of battle', or, in other words, of the way in which his units were disposed. This was thought to provide a clear idea of his intentions, whereas, more often than not, owing to the rapidity with which movements are carried out nowadays, the evidence thus gathered was susceptible of three or four mutually contradictory interpretations. To this, its main task, were added certain routine inquiries about morale and political conditions, and these were normally carried out by men who were obviously ignorant of the ABC of sociological analysis. I remember a leaflet purporting to provide inside information about influences at work in Belgium, which thought it had said all that was necessary when it had remarked, in the best *Almanach de Gotha* style, that the form of the kingdom was that of a 'Constitutional Monarchy'! How much that amounted to we were to learn from bitter experience!

As to the dissemination of information, it was a standing joke at most headquarters that, as soon as Intelligence found out anything, it proceeded to put it down on paper, mark the document in red ink 'Top Secret', and then shut it away from all those likely to be interested in its contents, in a safe with a triple lock. I had clear proof one day that this was not just a good story. I had got Intelligence to promise that it would circulate to the various Corps H.Q. the annotated list of Belgian fuel dumps which we had at long last managed to compile. A little later we had occasion to issue to senior formations a series of general instructions on the subject of indenting for fuel in the event of an advance into Belgium. It dealt first with the subject of requisitioning, passed on to describe the arrangements which would be made by First Army for setting up its own depots, and referred recipients for details about the whereabouts of local supplies to the table already circulated. In every case it was passed to 'Q'. On the very day of its publication I had a rather acid telephone call from my opposite number at Corps. 'You mention a Table.

No Table has come our way.' I at once instituted inquiries. The document had been duly dispatched. But, according to army rules and regulations, whenever instructions are issued by one particular section of the staff, they go, with the certainty of gravity, to the same section of the subordinate formation to which they are addressed, which, in this case, happened to be Intelligence. There our precious table had been immediately shut away in the famous secret safe, and no one had taken the trouble to pass on the information which it contained to the one officer capable of using it! My indignation was greeted by my colleagues with cynical shrugs: 'The same old story!' The question of putting the blame fairly and squarely on the shoulders of those responsible, or of taking steps to see that such mistakes should not occur in future, was never even considered. Army routine, apparently, was too deeply rooted to be disturbed.

Intelligence, with us, was far from being a model of organization, as we very well knew. Nevertheless, even the most hardened staff officer could not refrain from a faint surprise at some of the 'appreciations' issued during the period of waiting which preceded the German offensive. One particular railway map became famous. A mistake in the tracing had turned Aix-la-Chapelle into a Belgian city, and the main line from Hamburg to Berlin was shown as a 'branch' capable of carrying only light traffic! That, however, was not a very serious matter because the blunder was too obvious to deceive anybody. The 'Intelligence Summary', however, which appeared at brief intervals, contained fundamental errors which, in the event, were to have serious consequences. Consider, for a moment, what happens when anyone engaged on exact research sets about drawing up the balance-sheet of his discoveries—an archaeologist, for instance, publishing successive summaries of his finds, a doctor working over a case-entry with his pupils, or the kind of information confided by Pasteur to his famous 'working note-book'. What do we expect to find in such scientific documents? We rely on them to tell us, at each stage of the investigation under review, that some piece of evidence, till now lacking confirmation, has been proved correct; that some interpretation of the facts, formerly undisputed, must, in the light of subsequent discoveries, be henceforward discredited. Similarly, when it is not the past that we are studying, but some set of phenomena relating to a principle still active, we expect to be told whenever a new piece of evidence may emerge, in the light of which it is quite possible that the whole elaborate structure of our conclusions will have to be changed. In other words, knowledge being essentially a progressive movement of the intelligence, and knowledge of *events*, which by their very nature can never be static, being possible only when the graph of that movement can be constantly consulted, any *single* statement of results must always be valueless unless it can be compared with similar statements made at an earlier stage of the inquiry. Now these 'summaries' were circulated in series, without any attempt being made to stress the relationship between them. By studying them closely, one often came to realize that they were mutually contradictory, or that, having first underlined one particular group of facts as offering results rich in possibilities, a later issue would gaily relegate these same facts to oblivion without a word of warning or explanation. Were we to assume, then, that the later 'appreciation' entirely superseded the earlier? —that all reference to former information had been deliberately avoided?—that the whole situation had radically changed? It would have needed a very clever man to answer such questions. To be perfectly frank, I am not a little afraid of falling into the sin of calumny, because, more than once, I found myself wondering how much of this muddled thinking was due to lack of skill, how much to conscious guile. Every officer in charge of an Intelligence section lived in a state of constant terror that when the blow fell events might blow sky-high all the conclusions which he had told the general in command were 'absolutely certain'. To put before him a wide choice of mutually contradictory inferences ensured that no matter what might happen, one could say with an air of triumph—'If *only* you had listened to my advice!'[1]

What, precisely, was the value of the services rendered by Intelligence to the operational staff in the matter of day-to-day reports, once active fighting had begun? On that point I should be hard put to it to pronounce judgement, because no particulars of what was said or done ever reached me. But one thing is certain. The famous 'summaries' were, from then on, condemned to a silence as complete as it was prudent, with the result that those officers whose job resembled mine never got any information at all about the enemy, save what they were lucky enough to pick up in general conversation, or as the result of some chance meeting— in other words, almost exactly nil, or, at least, nil in comparison with what their, possibly idle, curiosity demanded in the way of mental sustenance, or with what they should most certainly have known if they were to carry out their duties efficiently. When, as occasionally happened, one did stumble on some fact of importance, one was left with no alternative (I have already quoted a specific instance), in the absence of any proper clearing-house, but to go straight to the army commander. Such odds and ends of Intelligence should, of course, be thoroughly arranged and digested before being presented to a commanding officer who has already got more on his plate than he can con-veniently absorb.

It is not enough that such centres or 'agencies'—to repeat my

[1] B. de Jouvenel, in his book, *La Décomposition de l'Europe libérale*, p. 212, has some crushing things to say about the bad habits of our Intelligence Service in the days before the war. 'Our General Staff shows a childish vanity in announc-ing through the medium of the League of Nations Year Book (*l'Annuaire militaire de la S.D.N.*) particulars of troops which, in fact, do not exist at all, of Regulars whose enlistment papers have never been received, of Reservists who have not been called to the colours. By doing this they merely bolster up the German argument.' See also, for 1914, Joffre's *Mémoires*, p. 249, where he makes reference to the faulty information which was given to him relative to the German Reserve Corps. (July 1942.)

former analogy—should be grouped into a single Intelligence Branch charged with both issuing and receiving information. Each section of the staff should contain at least one specialist officer whose whole duty it should be to sift and circulate all available 'news'. How could we possibly keep the forward units supplied with ammunition, food, engineers' stores, and fuel, or how could we establish munition dumps, rail-heads, sappers' dumps, or mobile supply columns, if half the time we did not know where the formations concerned were located, or how the enemy was moving?[1]

The faulty methods of work used by Intelligence, and by many other branches of the staff in all the armies, did not, for the most part, remain unnoticed by our senior generals, and I am pretty sure that among the latter and those working in close touch with them there were plenty of keen-sighted men who, in the intimacy of their own hearts, condemned this state of affairs. How came it, then, that no disciplinary action was ever taken, and that none of those responsible were removed from their posts? 'Punishment in the French Army is a thing of the past'— my young friends of the fighting formations said on more than one occasion. The generalization is, no doubt, crude, but there is more than a grain of truth in it. The whole question of 'authority' was passing through a period of crisis, and giving rise to a situation which must be analysed in greater detail.

[1] This weakness in the matter of Intelligence has long been a blemish on French Staff work. The Duc de Fezensac, in his *Mémoires*, records that, on one occasion, when he had been told by Ney to take certain orders to one of the Marshal's subordinate general officers, he asked where the latter was to be found. '... "No comments"—was the answer I got from the Marshal: "don't like 'em! ..." '— and Fezensac goes on to say—'We were never told where the troops were. No movement-orders, no situation-reports were ever shown to us. We had to find out as best we could, or, it would be truer to say, we had to guess.' (Quoted by M. Leroy in his *La Pensée de Sainte-Beuve*, p. 56.) You and I, Lachamp, could take that remark of Fezensac's, and apply it unaltered to our own case—could we not? (July 1942.)

At one time I saw a great deal of certain regimental officers. I do not doubt that now, as formerly, there are a great many fine fellows among them who are capable of running their units with justice and a tactful firmness as far removed, on the one hand, from easy-going slackness—the very idea of which is abhorrent to me—as from the absurd bullying methods of the legendary 'Barrack-Square fire-eater' on the other. There is no finer job than that of the company, battalion, or regimental commander when it is carried out with the high-mindedness which belongs of right to the French tradition. I have often noticed that it develops in men who have inherited the right attitude, those virtues of humanity for which I have the highest admiration. I am glad to say that I found them in that charming staff officer who was for some time second-in-command of our section before he moved on to more elevated spheres. 'Now *he's* gone', was the sad refrain of the orderly-room clerks, 'there'll be nobody to bother about *us*!' Only the stupid are afraid that sympathy may deteriorate into familiarity.

But from what I have heard—and I have no reason to disbelieve the stories—the control of large bodies of men did not always or everywhere show a similar degree of humane imagination. There are two phrases which I should like to see deleted from the soldier's vocabulary—'breaking in' and 'toeing the line'. They may have been all right for the soldiers of the Royal Sergeant Major,[1] but they have no place in a truly national army. Not that I wish to deny that even in a national army, perhaps *especially* in a national army, discipline is necessary, or that it has to be learned. But it should be an extension of civic virtue, and, as Pierre Hamp has so well said when speaking of true courage— 'an expression of the professional conscience'. I once heard an officer become eloquent over his surprise at the efficiency of the girl telephonists employed at the main Army switchboard. 'They do it as well as they would if they were *soldiers*!'—he said in a

[1] Presumably the reference is to Frederick the Great. (*Translator.*)

tone of voice which I could never hope to describe, so shaken was it with outraged amazement. How could a man so dominated by caste prejudice hope to be a successful commander of troops raised from the mass of the people for the defence of their country, men who, in civil life, had grown accustomed to the freedom of the family circle?

In practice, this business of 'toeing the line' is almost always confused with a forced respect for certain external marks of authority. Such respect, though not without value when it is the expression of a deep and sincere sense of hierarchy, cannot with profit be insisted upon except when a spirit of confidence has been created which is sufficiently strong to ensure that any act of public deference springs spontaneously from a genuine *wish* to show respect. I am prepared even to admit that men must be 'broken in', but only if that process takes into account their quality of human beings—as every true leader has always been ready to recognize. I should most certainly not apply the words 'true leader' to the colonel—and I believe this story to be true—who broke one of his N.C.O.s because, on one very cold day, he caught him with his hands in the pockets of his great-coat, and who insisted on having reports rendered to him at intervals during each day on the turn-out of his men, though he thought nothing of leaving them to freeze in the depths of winter in badly organized huts. I myself witnessed the effects produced by one such attempt at 'breaking in'. It was in Normandy, when we were being reorganized after the Flanders campaign. How willing, how profoundly 'decent', the men were at that time! Even the most hardened old sweat felt touched by the daily spectacle of their behaviour. They came to us straight from the trains, after an exhausting journey, often half-starved, sometimes with no clothes but the odd assortment of garments which the English had provided when they fished them out of the sea after the ship on which they were travelling had gone to the bottom. They had lost their units, their officers, their pals. Not infrequently they had walked miles before reaching a camp where they could find something of that atmosphere of mutual help and companionship which is so necessary a part of the soldier's life. Not one word of complaint did I hear. The least little thing we managed to do for them was accepted with a hearty 'Thank you, sir', which we found more than sufficient reward for any efforts we might have made. They were so pleased not only at being once more, if only temporarily, sheltered from the blast, but at discovering, too, that some officer, about whom they had been worrying, was safe and sound. Some of the handshakes that I got on that occasion warmed my heart. Indeed, the memory of those days would make it impossible for me ever to despair of the French people—assuming that I were otherwise tempted to do so.

I am sure that the general sent to command us meant well. There was no doubting the sincerity of his faith in the military virtues, and he was as hard on himself as he was on others. But he was deficient in psychological insight. He decided that the prevailing atmosphere was not that of a well-conducted barracks, and set about putting things to rights. The number of officers' inspections rapidly increased, and we began to be snowed up under an accumulation of reports reaching us from all sides on such subjects as defective pullovers. Fresh from what the newspapers were already rather pompously, but not altogether erroneously, calling the 'Hell of Flanders', some of us had planned to bring our wives to the villages in which we were billeted. Privates as well as officers were to have this privilege, and there was to be equality of treatment for all. The general came down on the idea like a ton of bricks. It was permissible, in his opinion, for a fighting soldier to go to the local brothel if he wanted to, but he maintained that the legitimate intimacies of married love would merely serve to weaken morale. He was a just man according to his lights, and he started the ball rolling by awarding fifteen days' close arrest to the elderly general of reserve who, up till then, had been in charge of us, because he had come on him one evening walking arm-in-arm with his equally elderly wife. We officers treated the whole thing as a huge joke. Not so the rank and file. In the course of a few days the whole moral tone of the camp had completely changed. A significant symptom of the deterioration was to be found in the fact that whereas the men had previously saluted with whole-hearted enthusiasm, they now did so grudgingly and obviously only because they had to. The so-called 'breaking in' had admirably succeeded, and in the shortest possible time, in completely ruining the fine, healthy attitude of soldiers who had recently emerged from the furnace of war, and would soon, or so we believed, be going back into it.

Several people I have met who lived, from 1914 to 1918, under German occupation, and have again been subjected to the same fate in recent months, have told me, quite independently of one another, something with which I have been greatly struck—that compared with the old Imperial army, the troops of the Nazi régime have the appearance of being far more 'democratic'. The gulf between officers and men seems now to be less unbridgeable (though, as I can testify from personal experience, the German officer of to-day has the same bad habit as his predecessor of never returning salutes in a proper manner). From highest to lowest there is a more clearly marked participation by all ranks in a general atmosphere of goodwill. That spiritual communion which is the outcome of the special brand of mysticism rife in modern Germany is extremely powerful, and we should not let the crudity of its origins blind us to that truth. It would be disastrous should our own national spirit be compromised by the dominance of old traditions modelled on those of the Prussian school, which, fundamentally, are so antipathetic to it, especially when in Prussia itself they are now held to be out of date.

For good or ill the old habits of punishment have certainly not been forgotten in the French Army. It might be better if they had been. It is only too obvious that our High Command did not, as it could and should have done, take advantage of the long period of waiting imposed upon it by the enemy to carry out much necessary purging of the personnel of the regular army. A few officers in the First Army were, to be sure, 'bowler-hatted' when active operations began, to the accompaniment of a considerable amount of publicity. But why had this disciplinary action been left to wait until the proper time for it had gone by? Glaring cases of incompetence had been notorious long before that date.

Here is another example of what I mean, should one be needed. Our D.A.Q.M.G. was an old officer whose utter unfitness for the job was not disguised by his rather childlike friendliness with all and sundry. 'For the last thirty years I've never really understood what it is I'm supposed to do', he loved to say. This frank admission was a standing joke with us, and I should be much surprised to discover that it had not percolated to the highest quarters. The duties of this deserving pupil of Captain Bravida did not, while we were at Bohain, amount to much. But it was pretty obvious that once active hostilities began, they would become a great deal more onerous. They included, officially, the organization of staff cars, which, both before and, unfortunately, after 10 May, left much to be desired. The retirement of an officer of his rank would not have involved anything like the same complications as the dismissal of the Commander-In-Chief, or even of an army commander. But this clown of a colonel was allowed to stay on, not only for the whole of the winter, but through all the subsequent campaign—though, incidentally, during the latter period we saw little or nothing of him—until the day when, just as he was about to embark at Dunkirk, he mysteriously disappeared. What happened to him? His end became a matter of legend. It is wiser to admit that nothing is known, and to assume—as, after all, is most likely—either that he just died for his country or was accidentally taken prisoner. It was certainly not his fault that he had been maintained in a post that had put too great a strain on his modest capabilities. Nor was he the only one in like case. Ruthlessness of the kind shown by Joffre in 1914 was conspicuous by its absence. We could have done with a few of his 'Young Turks'. Some of them were still alive. But by 1940 they were elderly men, weighed down with honours and spoiled by a lifetime of office-work and easy success. For the 'flabbiness' which was so evident in the High Command had its origin chiefly in habits of living contracted during the years of peace. The 'paper' mania, too, had a good deal to do with it. What would have happened if the senior Intelligence Officer who failed to pass on information of the first importance to the only man capable of using it had been at the head of one of the big departments of a private business concern? His boss would, I imagine, have sent for him, told him a few home truths behind locked doors, and sent him back to his office with a pretty threatening—'see it doesn't happen again'. And it probably would not have happened again. Very different were conditions in the Army, as I saw them. Had I wished to get the guilty party reprimanded by my immediate superior, by the Chief of Staff, or, in the last resort, by the army commander, I should have had to submit a complaint in writing. Worse still, this memorandum, in accordance with sacrosanct military tradition, would have had to be addressed to the corps commander, since communications between formations could be conducted only at the highest level. The whole business would thus have become a major 'incident'. The general tone of the advice given to me was that I had much better not get mixed up in a lot of fuss and bother. My report would have been successively watered down at each stage of its travels, and nothing at all would have happened about it even if, at long last, it *had* reached the august desk. Add to this the terror of 'making a nuisance of oneself', the mania for handling all such matters with kid gloves, which becomes second nature with men who are itching for promotion: the fear of annoying those who are powerful to-day or who may become powerful to-morrow. On one occasion, as a result of a suggestion of mine, it was decided to reduce the issue of petrol to one of the corps, and to increase that of another by the amount thus saved. This involved the sending out of two complementary sets of instructions. The Deputy Chief of Staff, who at that time was acting for his superior, got General Blanchard to sign the order limiting consumption, though he sent out over his own signature the letter which gave the second corps the good news that they might draw more liberally on the supplies available. In this way he managed to insinuate that the piece of bad news had nothing to do with him, but that he was wholly responsible for the good one. That is the way in which an officer seeks to assure his future. By making oneself party to a reprimand, one runs the risk of compromising one's chances. If one is not too sure of oneself, one certainly fears, rightly or wrongly, that they *may* be compromised. Routine is, by nature, elastic. Those bred up in army ways had, in the course of years spent in the bureaucratic machine, grown used to a certain amount of incompetence which rarely, if ever, ended tragically. Times changed, but not habits. To put the matter in a nutshell, one can say that staff experience under peace conditions did not provide a good training for character. The truth of that generalization turned out, in more ways than one, to be only too obvious.[1]

[1] The problem is a grave one. It is nowhere more clearly stated than in the first volume of Joffre's *Mémoires*. Among other disturbing items, the author prints the truly shattering list of general officers whom it was necessary to relieve of their duties during the early months of the war. (Between the date of mobilization and 6 September 1914 at least one-half of the divisional commanders on the active list were retired, and precisely the same proportion of the commanders of cavalry divisions.) Joffre's remark about a certain corps commander, that 'he was utterly incapable of adapting a peace-time mentality to the needs of war', was obviously true of most of the senior officers thus 'degummed'—in other words, of 50 per cent. of the peace-time generals. Of what use, one may ask, is a military education which trains men for everything except war? (July 1942.)

One of the Vanquished gives Evidence

There is an old army saying about the mutual feelings of any two officers who happen to be travelling together up the ladder of promotion. 'If they are Lieutenants, they are friends: if Captains, comrades: if Majors, colleagues: if Colonels, rivals: if Generals, enemies.' I leave the reader to decide whether I am in a position to speak with knowledge of the professional jealousy which formed the subject of so much covert gossip among my companions. Fanned to flame by the crowd of hangers-on inevitably surrounding each boss with a complexity of flattery and intrigue, it fed on the fuel that was only too prevalent in a system of multiple seniority. French Army authorities have never realized that the greater the number of layers that an order or a 'mem' has to penetrate in the course of its journey from point of origin to point of reception, the greater is the risk that it will never arrive in time. Worse still, where the number of senior officers is too large, responsibility becomes so diluted that it is never felt as an urgent personal preoccupation by any one of them. This defect of the military bureaucracy flourishes at every level. I have already made it clear that if we, who were concerned with the provision and distribution of fuel, had observed regulations to the letter, we should have found a staircase of three flights separating the representative of the army commander from the officers who actually had to carry out all instructions that were issued. Between the colonel of an infantry regiment and division stood the masking wall of the divisional staff, or, as we used to put it when I was a foot-slogger, a 'proper brake'. I should be surprised to learn that this nickname was any less applicable now than it was then. Higher still was a whole series of other formations—Army, Army-Group (in principle, a mere device to ensure strategic co-operation, though it frequently tried to free itself from this limitation), the Commander of the North-East Theatre of Operations—who was responsible for the conduct of hostilities on the whole of the French front, Alps excepted—and, finally, the Commander-in-

Chief of the land forces. At a time when a division of functions had been arranged between these last two—or, in ordinary human terms, between General Georges and General Gamelin— I was once present at a lecture staged by G.H.Q. with the object of explaining the new organization. The speaker made himself as clear as he knew how. I was not, however, the only one there who entirely failed to get any clear-cut idea of what he was trying to bring home to us. There was confusion and over-lapping at every turn: and it was inevitable that there should be. Various echoes that reached me later were proof that our fears had not been ill founded. And even so, we were reckoning with-out that third embryo of a Headquarters Staff, lying concealed in the innermost recesses of the temple—the Commander-in-Chief's Military Cabinet.

All this, however, was a world far removed from my own humble sphere. But I had many opportunities of judging at close range the rivalry that existed between the various sections of the High Command, and, in a more rarefied atmosphere, between the General Staff (in other words, G.H.Q.) and the General Staff of the Army as a whole (in other words, the War Office).

One of the most remarkable officers it was ever my good fortune to encounter—the lieutenant-colonel whose concern for our orderly-room clerks I have already mentioned—once said to me: 'There should never be any *branches* in a Headquarters Staff.' He meant by this that any such subdivision, though perhaps inevitable, was always fraught with danger. For each part or branch is almost bound to slip into the fallacy of sub-stituting itself for the whole, and the small enclosed world of the staff to regard itself as synonymous with the nation. 'G'— which is the home of the strategists, and was named by our more bitter wits 'The Brains Trust'—is normally regarded as the Holy of Holies. Proud of their function, which, it cannot be denied, is extremely important and delicate, the officers belonging to it are

97

not always careful to co-operate as closely as they should with those of their colleagues who partake less regularly of the pure milk of the military word. They even seem, at times, to treat with a certain degree of contempt those activities without which the lines and arrows traced on the operational maps would remain but empty symbols. The same is true, for other reasons, of Intelligence, whose members live in a world haunted by the spirit of secrecy. Not that the formal code of good manners is not, save by a few cantankerous characters, scrupulously observed. The fact remains, however, that a system of watertight compartments is universal in the higher reaches of the Army. Nowhere have I found them less penetrable than at the very top—G.H.Q. I once spent the whole of a January afternoon trying, unsuccessfully, to get Intelligence and 'Q' to agree on some sort of common action. The particular point at issue had to do, I need hardly say, with fuel supply—which meant that it was not wholly unimportant. Since it involved a number of persons whom I have no right to compromise, I must, in speaking of it, proceed rather circumspectly.

There was, in a small neutral country situated at about an equal distance from the French and German frontiers, a certain dump containing motor fuel and lubricants. The man on whom I usually relied for information had not merely given me details of the capacity (which was considerable) of the tanks, but had sent me the following message: 'I can, if you so wish, see to it that they are always kept filled to the maximum. This would make your supply problem easier in the event of your finding yourselves constrained, some day, to move your troops into the territory on which they are situated. Alternatively, I can maintain the bare minimum necessary for the requirements of peaceful commerce, thereby avoiding the danger of having to abandon valuable resources to the Germans. It is for the French General Staff to decide. As soon as I know what they want done, I will take the necessary steps.' The whole problem resolved itself into knowing whether, in the event of a German breach of neutrality, the High Command meant us or the enemy to reach this particular locality first. I was not competent to reach a decision on my own responsibility, for the Army holding this sector of the frontier was not the one to which I belonged, nor did it even form part of our 'Group'. There was nothing for it, therefore, but to ask G.H.Q. for orders. I went first to Intelligence, to which I had certain other pieces of information to impart. When I touched on the burning question, the gentlemen of that particular branch said, not without some show of plausibility—'Our job is to collect information, not to make decisions: go to "Q".' They did not, however, offer to go with me. Doubtless they had their reasons for not doing so. It would, I suppose, in any case have been more natural for me to go direct to the senior officer in charge of operations, or to one of his representatives. But it is scarcely fitting for one of the uninitiated to knock at the door of the sanctuary. So I was very soon on my way down the long street of la Ferté-sous-Jouarre, sown thick with military police, to the home of 'Q', with the intricacies of which branch I was, I need hardly say, already familiar. I was passed on from office to office. In each I heard the same formula: 'We don't know what the enemy may mean to do. *Our* job is to keep you supplied with *French* stuff. Besides, are you sure that this fellow is trustworthy? He may be trying to lead us into a trap.'

'Intelligence is prepared to guarantee the soundness of the information.'

'Oh, Intelligence! What's Intelligence got to do with fuel supplies? If they've started meddling in your affairs, they'd better go on.'

'That's all right by me. But if that's the line you've decided to take, I wish you'd give them a ring and tell them so.'

This they did, and I at least had the satisfaction of hearing what appeared to be a rather acid conversation. Each party to it seemed to be purely concerned with passing the buck. At the

99

end of a few minutes 'my' end terminated the exchange by observing drily—'that's not *our* business'. It was just like two householders quarrelling over a party-wall. The only things they neither of them seemed to be concerned about were the needs of the French Army as a whole. Being mulish by nature, I took the matter up again with 'Q'. My pilgrimage from department to department brought me finally into the presence of two lieutenant-colonels. I explained my mission with considerable warmth—with more warmth, probably, than was becoming in one of my relatively humble rank, but pulled myself up just in time not to overstep the bounds of hierarchic decency, and, since a scandal would have spelt irremediable disaster, said no more. But I felt thoroughly discouraged. All I had got for my pains was a vague promise that the point should be put to the Director of Supplies, who, no doubt, would consult his opposite number at 'G'. . . . They had made up their minds, it was clear, that the only way of getting rid of a tiresome and probably slightly unbalanced visitor was to *seem* to meet him half-way. As things turned out, I never heard another word about the affair.

All the same, I felt uncomfortable about not sending some sort of answer to the 'sympathizer' across the frontier who, in so disinterested a fashion, and at considerable risk to himself, had offered to help us. It was not only that the point he had raised was of considerable importance. Unbroken silence on our part would have betrayed to this foreigner the shilly-shallying state of mind of the French High Command. It was bad enough to know it ourselves. With the approval of the French friend (himself not a soldier) who had acted as inter-mediary, I sent the following message: 'Don't fill your tanks.' In doing this, I committed a terrible breach of discipline. In the event, however, I did not feel any high degree of guilt. The storm burst, and, as was only to be expected, the Germans beat us to it.

It was these inquiries of mine in the matter of the dump that put me wise to the struggle going on inside our own ranks, a struggle, as it were, on the side-lines of the far greater one which we were waging, or preparing to wage, against the Germans. In this secondary campaign, G.H.Q. was at grips with the War Office, la Ferté-sous-Jouarre with Paris. This particular form of tension was traditional and went back, probably, to the old days of Chantilly, when Joffre and Galliéni were the protagonists.

Our first attempts to find out something about Belgian fuel supplies had produced very incomplete results. The man from whom we had got our information was only too anxious to tell us more, but how could we let him know what it was that we wanted to find out? To ask him to go to Paris was out of the question, and he was not anxious to have dealings with the Military Attaché, whose visits might have compromised him, or with secret agents, who are more used to dealing with mercenary informers than honest merchants, and had not, in any case, the special knowledge which they would have needed in order to discuss matters of fuel supply. The simplest solution of the difficulty, it seemed to me, would be for our French intermediary to go to Brussels under cover of a business trip. That, too, was the opinion of Army Group Intelligence, who were taking great interest in the matter. All that remained was to get the necessary visas for our willing helper. The mission would involve him in considerable self-sacrifice and loss of time. We did not want to add to his difficulties by making him kick his heels in police-stations and embassy waiting-rooms. The thing *seemed* easy enough. Not only had I the best of reasons for being able to answer for the reliability of a man whom I knew intimately, but he was well known and highly esteemed in Paris commercial circles, and was already in close touch with the military authorities. Finally, Army Group and, at a still higher level, G.H.Q. were prepared to back his credentials. Nevertheless, the necessary formalities would have to be completed through the Intelligence department of the War Office. In spite of the categorical recommendations of Army Group (which was speaking in the name of G.H.Q. as well as in its own), and perhaps because of them, the War Office flatly refused to listen. 'We don't know this fellow', they said, 'and we have no idea what it is he proposes to do' (useless to point out that they had been fully informed on this point). 'We can take no responsibility. He must straighten things out for himself.' This he did, at the cost of many tedious delays, though, fortunately, owing to his personal contacts, they were not as complicated as they might otherwise have been. But the incident as a whole taught me that we had to deal, not with the French Army, but with a series of jealously guarded preserves within it.

I was to be brought up, still more blatantly, and in far more tragic circumstances, against this same fact when the necessity arose, in Normandy, of reconstituting a show of armed might out of the flotsam and jetsam saved from Flanders. Not only were we passed on from general to general, some of whom changed in the course of a single day, and all of whom, as soon as they entered on their functions, set about undoing what their predecessors had begun; the bitter quarrel between G.H.Q. and the War Office went on all the time over our heads and at our expense, or, rather, at the expense of the nation. In theory, at least, in those early days we took our orders from the second of these bodies, because Normandy was regarded in the light of a remote back-area (though, in fact, at that time the front was on the Somme), far removed from the Army zones. I need not stress the truth that this duel was not exactly helpful to us in our task of reorganization and re-equipping. The enemy was literally at the gates of the city—if, indeed, he was not already within them—but that made not the slightest difference to our internecine strife. The fact that the struggle was one between, not political parties, but parties belonging to the same army, made the whole business much less easy to forgive.

For the man who chooses the career of arms, personal courage is by far the most necessary of all professional virtues. So indispensable is it to the morale of the troops, that no one dreams of questioning its presence. I am quite certain that the great majority of regular officers are true to this splendid tradition. If, here and there, exceptions to the rule have been found—I came across one or two in the course of the last war, and have a suspicion that I met a few in this one—they do not in any way besmirch the honour of the Army as a whole. They merely prove that the habit does not always make the monk, and also that in all countries and at all times there are men so lacking in imagination that they will choose an occupation without realizing what it involves. They will, for instance, elect to become soldiers without considering that, sooner or later, they may have to change the peaceful life of a garrison town for war. Weaklings of this kind are really nothing but self-deceived unfortunates. But, leaving these extreme cases aside, it is important to grasp the fact that the contempt of danger takes many different forms and may be present in many different degrees. It is impossible to go deeply into the problem without finding oneself brought up against certain shameful secrets tucked away in the obscure recesses of one's own memory. Anybody who has ever been under fire will know what I mean. Even the most hardened warrior is at times hard put to it to control his nerves, though there are occasions when the same man will show himself, without apparent effort, wholly indifferent to personal risk. His bravery has the appearance of being an immediate and automatic reflex—the result of habit, or, quite simply, of a well-organized nervous system. But courage is not confined to any one profession or to any one caste. Experience gained in two wars—and, particularly, in that of 1914–18—leads me to the conclusion that it is the common property of all healthy human beings—at least, in France, whose people have, for the most part, a plentiful supply of sound sense and well-knit bodies. It is a popular fallacy

103

among officers that the man of hot temper, the adventurer or the hooligan, makes the best soldier. That is far from being the truth. I have always noticed that the brutal temperament is apt to break under the strain of prolonged danger. Courage, after all, is the soldier's job, and the ordinary, decent man is in the habit of doing his daily work conscientiously and properly, whether it be at the bench, in the fields, behind the counter, or, if I may be allowed to say so, at the desk or in the laboratory. He will carry on, without fuss, with what he has got to do, even when bombs are falling and bullets are flying, particularly where a sense of solidarity with others is added to his natural instinct for getting the task finished. This sense may find expression in many different ways. It may take the form of a more or less irrational resolve not to leave a pal in the lurch, or the perfectly conscious determination to sacrifice personal considerations to the interests of the nation. But the cruder forms of courage lead, by almost imperceptible degrees, to the higher. I have never come across better fighters than the miners of the Nord and the Pas de Calais whom I saw at close quarters in the first war. I found only one exception to this rule, and for a long time it puzzled me, until I discovered, quite by chance, that the man in question was a 'scab', by which I mean a non-unionist employed as a strike-breaker. It is not a question of party politics. Quite simply, it comes to this: that where, in times of peace, class-loyalty is absent, the ability to put selfish interests last fails inevitably on the field of battle. Most of the rank and file, and many of the officers, who made up the infantry who fought at Verdun and on the Somme, were reservists, and so, too, more recently, were my colleagues of the supply columns, the men who drove the mobile fuel containers, and so often, without a moment's thought for the danger they were running, would set fire to loads of petrol drums in an endeavour to keep them out of the enemy's hands: the men who supplied the tanks at a time when the line was so fluid that quite often they could not pack up, but had to dash back with the containers bumping along behind the tractors, and all their feed-pipes hanging out. These men were officially classed as 'second line' troops, and were, for the most part, unarmed. I have a vivid memory of one great-hearted chap, a chauffeur in civil life, who was mortally wounded in one of these refuelling operations, but obstinately refused to be picked up. 'I've had it,' he said; 'Get to hell out of this! I don't want any of my pals to be done in just because of me!' In the course of those now far distant four years of 1914–18— and for me they will always be the 'real' war—I saw many such cases of courage. About them I shall say no more. If I let myself go, I could talk on for ever.

A great deal has been said in recent months about cases of cowardice among the troops, and especially among the officers. Stories have been told of headlong flight with the commander's car out-stripping the rest of the field. Instances have been quoted of positions that were abandoned. There have been rumours that 'every man for himself' orders were issued by responsible authorities. I never, myself, witnessed these things, but one can account for the growth of a legend without being personally involved in its development. When a people has been defeated it always tries to smell out a traitor or two, or, at least, to find a few scapegoats on whom to fasten the responsibility for what has occurred. Still, let us admit (as I fear we must do) that such stories were not wholly groundless, that, as I have often heard my friends on the staff say, discipline at the front did break down. If that is so, then I think that the High Command was very largely to blame.[1]

---

[1] I have sifted a good deal of evidence in the course of the last two years, and am inclined to believe that these cases of cowardice in high places were not so rare as we should like to think—after, that is, it became obvious that we had been beaten. I have left the text of this part of my book as I originally wrote it, but, in the interests of strict truth, I ought, I fear, to stress this fact. The admission is painful, and I make it very unwillingly. There can be little doubt that morale was very shaky in certain call-up groups (and this applies as much to the regular as to

The lower and middle commissioned ranks of the fighting formations were, to a very large extent, filled by elderly men who, in the years immediately preceding the outbreak of war, had been serving as garrison officers. Now, whatever some people may think, the illusion is still widely prevalent that constant inspections, peace-time exercises, and the hundred and one trivia of regimental duties are good training for those who will be called upon to lead men under conditions of active warfare in which ordinary day-to-day routine cannot be relied upon to bolster up authority. In actual fact the qualities necessary for success in the field are often better learned in many civilian occupations, because they, at least, do teach men to shoulder responsibilities and to adapt themselves to changing circumstances. Add to this the relaxing atmosphere which prevails in a world of minor officialdom—for this, after all, and questions of prestige apart, is what the life of many company and battalion commanders in time of peace amounts to. Only the genuine enthusiast, or the man with a strong sense of duty, is rendered immune to the poison, and such do not make up the bulk of any army. The period of waiting which lasted until 10 May was quite long enough for the authorities to have carried out the necessary changes, and to have set flowing that new blood which was so essential. There is no better protection against a hardening of the mental arteries than adaptable minds and physical keenness. Captain Coignet and his pupils of the Napoleonic Wars may not have been geniuses, but at least they were young. The German Army, too, even from the little we saw of it, gave, in comparison with our own, an impression of youthfulness. It soon became

the reserve officers)—more shaky, indeed, than we once thought. But if that is so, it is no less true that the infection was far from being general. In the very circles which produced these instances of cowardice there were many acts of true heroism. It is such contrasts that make the writing of history so difficult. Similarly, we know only too well that the morale of the nation as a whole left much to be desired, and have seen how the morbid elements in the body politic reacted to the crisis. In this matter 'collaboration' has provided a sure touchstone. (July 1942.)

perfectly obvious that the French military authorities had no intention whatever of putting through the needful pruning opera-tions, nor were they sufficiently energetic in giving junior com-missions (even if it meant having a certain number of subalterns supplementary to establishment) to those reserve N.C.O.s who had been proved by the events of 1914 to have admirable qualities of initiative, loyalty, and command. I know many cases in which colonels stopped such men from applying for commissions because they thought that they were too valuable to lose, or because (I am sorry to say) the candidates were not able to pull enough strings. It may have been assumed that the weeding-out process would get going automatically in the course of the fight-ing, but if that was so, then those responsible forgot that the war might very well not last for four years. They never dreamed that, in fact, it would be over in less time than was occupied, in 1914, by the 'race to the sea'.

I have already laid sufficient stress on the effects of surprise. I use the word in its strictly strategic sense. The worst cases of mental paralysis were the result of that mood of outraged amaze-ment which laid hold of men who were faced by a rhythm of events entirely different from the kind of thing that they had been led to expect. From this form of psychological shock the officers of front-line formations were certainly not immune, but its ravages were most obvious farther back. There, as every-where else, men could be found with sufficient determination to stand up even to the test of the unexpected, and I know of one town-major, wounded in the last war, who volunteered to go forward in an attempt to disengage a detachment of tanks. But unfortunately, the inevitable withdrawal of the front assumed, only too often, the character of a headlong flight, which, in some instances, developed even before the enemy had attacked. On one occasion G.H.Q. had to order back to his post the com-mander of a military region after he had abandoned, without instructions, the town in which his headquarters were situated.

He gave as his reason for having done so the excuse that he thought the Germans were too close! Weaknesses of this kind (and there are other examples) most certainly deserve to be condemned, though one cannot help feeling a certain amount of pity for the guilty parties. In other circumstances the men concerned would probably have acquitted themselves honourably enough. Unfortunately, Fate had placed them in positions where daily routine was but an extension of their peace-time habits. The mental atmosphere in which they moved had the stuffy quality of the office and the back area. They had long lived in the conviction that the terms of their service would keep them from the 'front'. But the enemy broke the contract. Why had not somebody made it clear to these decent, conscientious men, most of whom were rather too old to be in harness, that in a war of movement there is always the risk that what to-day is the rear may turn out to-morrow to be the front?

The worst feature of the whole thing was that this shakiness invaded the circles of those who had serious responsibilities to shoulder. Many of us were in a position to see with terror how appallingly quickly, almost overnight, it laid hold on certain officers who exercised the highest functions of the staff, and notably on those who were in charge of operations. The first symptoms of the disease were external—haggard eyes, badly shaven chins, a nervous restlessness which showed itself, in the early stages, as a feverish irritability over small things, and went on to assume the form of a forced calmness which deceived nobody. When a high-ranking officer started to say 'What's the use?' it was time for the fighting troops to keep their eyes skinned. Very soon after that, the tide of despair began to rise, and, instead of stimulating men to renewed efforts, set them looking for refuge in a sort of nerveless, do-nothing apathy. I have seldom witnessed a more demoralizing spectacle than that of the way in which certain members of the 'G' branch seemed to slump. There were times, of course, when they would clutch at the most unlikely straws, especially when the initiative of rescue was to come not from themselves but others. One whole day at Attiches stands out in my memory as having been filled with intoxicating optimism bred of a quite unfounded belief that a relieving army was advancing by forced marches on Arras and Bapaume. But these spasms of hope were followed by a still deeper drop in the temperature of determination. In this matter the high and mighty gave us the worst possible example. 'Do anything you like, sir, but for Heaven's sake do something!' In those words, according to one of my colleagues who was present, a corps commander on one occasion addressed General Blanchard at Lens.

I was to hear even worse things. No doubt I was indiscreet, though my intentions were innocent enough. The cause of the trouble lay in my nocturnal habits. All through the campaign I flatly refused to sleep in cellars, though not from any desire to gain a reputation for bravery. My refusal was carefully argued and had, I think, a basis of sound common sense, being founded upon a calculation of probabilities. I am, unfortunately, extremely prone to rheumatism. The chances that a night spent in the damp would leave me completely crippled were, I reckoned, about 90 per cent., whereas the risk of a direct hit on our head-quarters building was considerably less. Besides, it was not always easy for me to find a convenient funk-hole. Ever since Lens we had been using stretchers instead of beds, and at the Château of Attiches I at first had mine put in my office on the ground floor. The choice, as things turned out, was unfortunate. Although I was not supposed to be on duty, it happened, two nights running, that generals, coming into the room and finding me there, woke me up to give them some item of information or to ask for guidance through the labyrinth of passages. I could hardly lie there and say, 'Ask the next chap: this is my night off.'

On the third night, which was that of 25/6 May, I decided to do better. There was a whole series of bedrooms on the first floor reserved for senior officers, but between them ran a corridor which might be regarded as unoccupied. I had my stretcher carried upstairs, and, as soon as my work was finished, which, as a rule, was very late, went up to snatch a few hours' rest.

I was awakened very early next morning by the closing of a door and the sound of voices. Someone had just gone into the adjoining room and was carrying on a conversation with its occupant. Neither of the two speakers took the slightest trouble to lower his voice. To this day I do not know who the visitor was, but I am quite certain that he was somebody of exalted rank. His voice was unfamiliar to me, though I recognized only too well that of his companion. There could be no doubt that it was General Blanchard's. In any case, the nature of their discussion would have served to remove any uncertainty I might have had on that point. In my innocence and my concern merely to find somewhere protected from draughts, I had snuggled down on the very threshold of the one room which I ought to have avoided like the plague. By the time I realized what was going on, it was too late to make my presence known. I could scarcely admit that I had accidentally overheard what was being said. Though I detest lying in any form, there was nothing for it but to pretend that I was asleep. Not that I had to do any such thing as it turned out, because no one discovered me. Meanwhile, the dialogue continued. I did not understand all of it, and, indeed, did not particularly try to. Much of what reached my ears I have forgotten. But there is one thing of which I am sure, absolutely sure, so sure that no amount of denial could ever shake my certainty. I distinctly heard General Blanchard say, more calmly than I could ever have thought possible: 'I haven't much doubt what's going to happen—double capitulation!' At that time it was only 26 May, and we had the means, if not of saving ourselves, at least of putting up a long, heroic, and desperate resistance, as whole islands of men had done in 1918 when they

were surrounded on the Champagne front, and so of containing
and exhausting a large number of German divisions. For days
afterwards I carried the general's words in my mind. They were
a heavy secret, all the heavier because I could share them with
nobody. They gave me the shudders: they still do.

It is this spectre—now for once brought into the clear light
of day—which has lain like a terrible shadow on the death-
agonies of our armies in Flanders, nay, more, on all the French
armies wherever found. 'Capitulation'—a word that no true
national leader would ever have brought himself to utter, even
in the strictest confidence; a word that he would not even have
thought. Nor would any true leader have spoken, as did a
Marshal of France, till then aureoled with glory, on 17 June, of
'asking for a cessation of hostilities' before, well before, he even
knew the terms on which such a request would be granted.
When one of my friends, a man of outstanding bravery, heard
that famous and mournful pronouncement he said to me: 'I
should say that both you and I are pretty sure of ourselves. But
it will be very difficult now to resist the temptation not to expose
ourselves unduly. For what can be more tormenting than the
fear of being killed at the very finish of a war? What sort of
stomach for the fight is the average soldier going to have now?'
What, probably, more than anything else marks the true leader
is the power to clench his teeth and hang on, the ability to impart
to others a confidence that he feels himself. This he can do only
if he *does* feel it. Never, until the very last moment, must he
despair of his own genius. Above all, he must be willing to
accept for the men under him, no less than for himself, sacrifices
which may be productive of good, rather than a shameful yielding which must remain for ever useless. History tells us of men
who were neither fools nor, in the matter of personal danger,
cowards, but who, for all that, succumbed to misfortune, and on
them its verdict has ever been one of contempt. 'When I see
what is going on all round us, I understand the behaviour of

Dupont at Baylen, and of Bazaine at Metz.' That terrible sentence was spoken in my hearing towards the end of May by a young regimental officer. He should have limited his historical analogy to Bazaine, if it is true, as subsequent events seem to have proved, that the ultimate abandonment of all effort was due as much to party bias and base political ambitions as to momentary discouragement. In 1940 the spirit of Bazaine triumphed.

If a leader is to stand firm against the onset of events, he needs, above all else, a healthy mind in a tough body. Bazaine was not only a politician, he was a worn-out man. The rapid collapse of morale in the High Command was, to a very large extent, due to the bad physical conditions in which its members worked. Even in the early days at Valenciennes, when the situation, though admittedly serious, gave no cause for despair, many officers whose duty it was to make decisions of the highest importance suffered from too little sleep, hasty meals, and the lack of proper routine. They spent their days in rushing from office to office, producing mountains of paper, and never giving themselves a chance to think things out quietly. Unhurried planning alone could have saved us. No doubt they thought that by allowing themselves to become martyrs to their nerves they were giving proof of a fine stoicism, just as by living in a continual rush they produced in their own minds an illusion of activity. They forgot that nerves always take their revenge, and that there can be no fruitful activity where there is no discipline of mind. Staff circles have always, even in time of peace, been over-fond of living in a perpetual atmosphere of fuss. They should have established, well in advance, a proper time-table of work. It would, of course, have had to be sufficiently elastic to meet the demands of battle, but some such fixed time-table ought to have been the ideal at which they aimed. Soldiers have always held up as a fine example old Joffre's habit of, no matter what the circumstances, having a good night's sleep. How much better it would have been if *our* leaders had taken a leaf out of his book.

What, however, it all comes back to, I am convinced, is that the system of education in which senior officers were trained was wholly wrong. They lacked toughness of fibre because their minds had not been properly conditioned. Several times, in the course of two wars separated by more than twenty years, I have heard senior officers, referring to the methods of training in which they were brought up, say, 'The Staff College taught us all wrong.' Not that its lessons had always been the same. Nothing in 1939, I am sure, was more alien to our leaders' minds than the military doctrine of Grandmaison—'that criminal', as I heard one of them exclaim—which was so dear to the strategists of 1914. They were far from despising the value of heavy artillery, nor did they any longer believe in bayonet charges against fortified positions, or in the theory of the offensive at all costs. But no matter how much the things taught may have changed, the method of teaching them was the same, and that is what really matters.

Captain T . . ., a sceptic if ever there was one, but, for all that, a born leader, was never tired of inveighing comically against the 'general ideas' a respect for which had been the main tenet of the creed with which his professors at the Staff College had tried to imbue him. 'There are no such things as general ideas.' I am not prepared to defend this contention, but what *is* true, and what Captain T . . . meant, is that in the field of the positive and technical sciences, ideas are of value only in so far as they mirror or sum up the concrete facts of a situation. If they do not do that they remain mere verbal counters having no connexion with actuality. Now every educationist knows well, and an historian perhaps better than most, that there can be no greater danger in teaching than to let words usurp the place of facts. That mistake is all the more fatal when one remembers that the young are temperamentally only too prone to become intoxicated by words, and to give them the validity of things. Just because staff officers are the intellectuals of the Army, and, knowing it, inclined to assume airs of superiority, they are—or so I have found it—more than most men, susceptible to ready-made formulae. There was, for instance, my old colonel, a man who had done brilliantly at the Staff College. I remember how, in 1916, when we were on our way up to the line previous to taking part in an offensive from which he was destined never to return, he said to me: 'It's a terrible thing to have to fight a war in one's own country', and then, hurriedly correcting himself, 'not that it really matters *where* a war is fought. A soldier's first duty is to destroy the enemy wherever found.' Our ruined crops, our factories in the enemy's hands, our mineral resources employed in turning out guns for the Germans—all these things ceased to matter to him once he could take refuge in a text-book dictum. In the best pages of a terribly uneven work, Taine has shown that the main characteristic of Napoleon's genius was his power of always being able to see the truth behind the appearance. I am afraid that our modern successors of Napoleon have lost this sovereign art. At Rennes, on 17 June, our High Command fancied that they were still exercising it, when all they were really doing was to succumb to the heady influence of the word 'position'.

When a lesson has been merely learned *passively*, its effects are apt to be fleeting. What one has to *teach* strikes deeper roots into the mind. Scarcely one of our leaders, or the colleagues with whom I worked, but had, at some time or other, and more or less frequently, gone back to the college as an instructor. Of all the sports practised in the Army, the sport of schoolmastering is the most popular, whether it takes the form of lecturing junior N.C.O.s or enunciating learned theories to candidates for the staff. The Corps of Officers is a humming pedagogic hive. Since I myself belong to the teaching profession, and have been instructing others for a good deal longer, alas, than I care to remember, I can rightly claim to have an opinion on such matters, and my opinion is that one should always treat the utterances of old schoolmasters with caution. They are forced by the circumstances of their job to amass a whole collection of verbal patterns, and on these they come, in the long run, to depend, as on so many secure nails, many of which are not wholly free from rust. Furthermore, being men of faith and doctrine, they are inclined, though without always realizing it, to favour the docile pupil at the expense of the aggressive sceptic. Very few of them keep their minds supple enough to retain the power of criticizing their own prejudices. Few of them succeed in escaping altogether the pitfalls of their calling. This is always dangerous, and particularly so when their listeners are also their subordinates in rank. For then contradiction is interpreted as indiscipline. The upper reaches of the staff swarmed, in my day, with former professors, and most of the operational chiefs were men who had once figured among their most promising pupils. These were not the best conditions, perhaps, in which to learn adaptability to new situations.

I am fully aware that Staff-College pupils had to learn a great many subjects. I have handled many of the official syllabuses and know how crammed they are with figures, calculations, details of artillery ranging and fuel consumption—matters, all of them, I do not doubt, of the highest possible importance. They were, as a rule, very thoroughly mastered. But there was, in addition, the War-Game, the indispensable, the dangerous War-Game—how dangerous one realizes only when one has seen teachers and pupils alike handling bodies of troops on the map with the help of a comforting array of multicoloured arrows. It needs an extremely imaginative mind to keep fast hold of the *facts* behind the symbols, to see and feel the reality of all the discomforts that beset the slowly marching column, the many incidents that may occur when troops are on the move, the effect of artillery fire, the frustration of inevitable delays, the misery caused when hot food is not ready at the right time, the embarrassments that may occur when guides lose their way or generals their heads. Only the most elastic of minds can make sufficient allowance for the unexpected—which means, in most cases, for what the enemy will do.

For the enemy is for the strategist a constant headache, and obviously, every soldier is primarily concerned with trying to anticipate his movements and, thereby, to counter them. Unfortunately, in this war, as formerly in 1914 or again in the spring of 1917 just before the Nivelles offensive, the enemy, because we had never learned enough about him, rarely did what we expected him to do. I do not think that this was chiefly due to any lack of prevision on our part. On the contrary, our prevision was almost too detailed. The trouble was that it covered only a limited number of possibilities. God knows, we had worked hard enough at perfecting 'Operation Dyle'. My own part in the planning was modest enough, but I could still explain in detail—if my files had not been burned—precisely how my fuel dumps in Belgium were to be organized on Zero-plus-9. What had not been foreseen was that when Zero-plus-9 arrived, I should no longer have any fuel dumps in Belgium, and precious few in our own back areas—and for a very good reason. The chief defect of the system lay in the fact that officers had been taught at peace-time lectures to attach too much importance to *manœuvre* and to theoretical tactics: in other words, to *book*-knowledge. Unconsciously they had got into the habit of expecting that everything would happen as the manuals said it would. When the Germans refused to play the game according to Staff-College rules, they found themselves as much at sea as the public speaker who is faced by questions to which he has not been taught the answers. They thought that everything was lost, and, therefore, acquiesced in the loss. When one has become too much fuddled by words and theories, the only safe guide is a sense of the *facts*, a power to make decisions, and an ability to improvise. It is precisely those things that a too hard-and-fast method of training fails to inculcate.

What strategical training in all countries needs and rarely gets is a sound basis of actuality. This can be found only in the lessons of history. How could it be otherwise? The military art is one of those technical subjects that precludes the possibility of experiment. The man who designs a new type of motor-car and wants to see how his ideas are likely to work out has only to construct a model. But what happens when a professor of the art of war wants to study the behaviour of two armies of a given type on the battlefield? He can scarcely mobilize tens of thousands of men, organize them according to his theories, and set them to butcher one another. There are, of course, manœuvres, but just because no one gets killed in these 'miniature wars'—as they used to be called—they give a completely distorted view of actual warfare. The more they are made to resemble the 'real thing', the more grotesque, as a rule, are the results. In these circumstances, the only sensible thing is to fall back on the lessons of the past, and to learn from them what, in other fields, we should find out by experimenting.

Is it fair to hold history responsible for the weaknesses of our strategic planning? It has sometimes been asked whether the lessons of history have not led us astray. I heard that doubt expressed by a young officer, recently graduated from the Staff College, at the end of our stay in Normandy, when the dark shadow of defeat was already upon us. If, by voicing it, he meant to question the value of the so-called history lessons he had received, I have no quarrel with his scepticism. But this teaching never, really, had anything to do with history. It was, if I may say so, at the very opposite pole from the science it was supposed to be inculcating. History is, in its essentials, the science of change. It knows and it teaches that it is impossible to find two events that are ever exactly alike, because the conditions from which they spring are never identical. I do not mean to deny that it recognizes certain elements in the evolution of mankind which, though not permanent, are extremely long-lived. But even while it lays this down, it has to admit that the possible number of their combinations is almost infinite. It realizes, properly enough, that successive civilizations show certain repetitive patterns, and that these resemble one another in their general lines, if not in their details, when the conditions determining them may be said to have a family likeness. It can even try to see into the future, and not always, I think, unsuccessfully. But the lesson it teaches is not that what happened yesterday will necessarily happen to-morrow, or that the past will go on reproducing itself. By examining how and why yesterday differed from the day before, it can reach conclusions which will enable it to foresee how to-morrow will differ from yesterday. The traces left by past events never move in a straight line, but in a curve that can be extended into the future. It matters not at all that the very nature of its subject-matter forbids the sort of experimentation which is possible in other fields of science. Observation and analysis enable it to establish the relations obtaining between events which are complicated by a whole series of surface variations. It establishes, by its study of them, a science of causes, and traces the different effects those causes may produce. History is, in the truest sense, an experimental science, because, by studying real events, and by bringing intelligence to bear on problems of analytical comparison, it succeeds in discovering, with ever-increasing accuracy, the parallel movements of cause and effect. The physicist does not say, 'Oxygen is a gas because we never come across it in any other form'; what he says is: 'Oxygen, in the conditions of temperature and pressure which most generally obtain in the atmosphere of our universe, shows itself in gaseous form.' Similarly, the historian is well aware that no two successive wars are ever the same war, because, in the period between them, a number of modifications have occurred in the social structures of the countries concerned, in the progress of technical skill, and in the minds of men.

No worse charge can be brought against the teaching of

history as almost invariably practised in our military schools than this—that it persuaded our army leaders of 1914 to expect the war then imminent to resemble the wars fought by Napoleon, and those of twenty-five years later that the war of 1939 would be a repetition of the war of 1914. I once glanced through the famous lectures delivered by Foch round about—if my memory is correct—the year 1910. Rarely has any book so thoroughly upset me. I do not deny that his analysis of Napoleonic tactics was admirable. But he did not stop at analysing them. He exhibited them as models to be followed irrespective of any changes that might have taken place in the world since Napoleon's day. He may, here and there, have made a passing reference to differences in armament and changes in topography. But such mild comments are not enough. Before embarking on any of his descriptions he should have uttered a loud note of warning. 'For Heaven's sake'—he should have told his audience—'don't rush to conclusions. I am about to analyse in detail battles that were fought over ground which had fewer roads than you would find in it to-day. And over such roads as there were transport moved at a speed which had scarcely, if at all, increased since medieval times. The fire-strength of the opposing armies was tiny compared with what we, to-day, can produce, and the bayonet was still the queen of weapons because neither the machine-gun nor barbed wire had then been invented. If we can still draw lessons from these actions, they will be of value only if you remember that wherever such new factors as I have mentioned play a part, the experience of an earlier day, when they were unknown, is worth almost nothing at all.' I have, I confess, only a very superficial acquaintance with the published works and spoken words of Foch's successors, but what little I do know of them bears out my suspicion that the spirit of their teaching has not noticeably changed.

Still, the High Command of 1914 did become the High Command of 1918. In spite of many bloody errors it learned to modify its methods and to adapt them to changing circumstance. Early in 1918 General Gouraud, an enthusiastic and ingenious educator, paraded two companies of infantry before a mixed class of officers, of whom I was one. The first of these two companies was equipped with the weapons, and performed the evolutions, of 1914. The other was of an entirely new type, armed, organized, and handled in accordance with the latest theories. The contrast was startling. But what was shown us that day was but an example taken from a fairly low stratum of the military pyramid. Actually, the change-over in method had brought about a revolutionary change in almost the entire conduct of war. How came it, then, that our leaders of 1940 were incapable of showing the same willingness to learn in the hard school of fact?

It would be foolish, in this connexion, to ignore the striking difference in duration which marked the two historical events of which I am speaking. Is it fair to expect that in a war of rapid movement men will have time to learn the lessons of their initial mistakes? The military authorities of 1914–18 were given a breathing-space of four years. We had only a few weeks. It would have needed a man of outstanding genius to change the whole conception of his strategy after the battle had been joined, and even had such a genius been available, the material ready to his hand would have made any such drastic action impossible. No, the new elements of the strategic problem should have been taken to heart *before* the outbreak of hostilities. But for most men the amount of intellectual effort involved in adapting themselves, in advance, to a set of circumstances conjured up merely as the result of a shrewd analysis of a given situation, is probably far greater and more difficult of achievement than the practical reorientation forced upon them *empirically* by the necessities of a concrete set of facts.

This, however, does not explain everything, and, as an excuse, it is insufficient. No one will readily believe that we had remained, all through the period of peace, in complete ignorance of what was happening in the German Army, or of the theories on which it was being trained. Besides, we had had before our eyes, ever since the summer of 1939, the practical lessons of the Polish campaign. They were clear, simple, and relevant. For what the Germans did later in the West was precisely what they had done earlier in the East. They made us a present of eight months of inactivity, and those eight months should have been used by us in thinking out afresh the whole strategic problem and in putting through the necessary reforms. We failed to take advantage of this opportunity. Why? Before making any effort to answer that question, I must make brief reference to a human and psychological factor of no little importance.

Who *were* our leaders in 1940? Corps and army commanders who had fought the last war in charge of battalions and regiments. Who were their chief assistants?—men who had commanded companies in 1918. All these officers had remained, though not always to the same extent, dominated by their memories of the *last* war. Nor can that be wondered at. Not only had they relived those glorious days a hundred times in books or lectures: not only had they based on them a whole curriculum of military education. They were soaked in them to the very marrow of their bones. Thoughts of the last war clung to them because they were the thoughts of their youth. Those long dead days had all the brilliance of things *seen*. A chord was struck in the minds of those men which called forth a resonant echo from the emotional recollection of their past. Incidents which, for others, served merely to illustrate some objective lesson in strategy were, for them, as for all of us who had known those years of fighting, unforgettable reminders of personal dangers faced and overcome, of friends killed at our side, of the fury we had felt at orders badly drafted, of the intoxication which had taken hold of us when we saw the enemy in flight. Many of them must, in 1915 or 1917, have led their men over the top in attacks on trenches which our guns had failed to flatten. They had only to close their eyes to see again the bodies caught in the wire and riddled with machine-gun bullets. A little later, promoted to the staff, they had helped to plan those cumbersome and carefully thought-out operations which, one day, were to end in victory—the winning of the Malmaison plateau which had been, as it were, the testing-ground for new and revolutionary tactics; Gouraud's defence in depth on 15 July 1918. Ill prepared by the instructions they had received or had given to others, to understand, instinctively, the working of the irresistible law of change, only a rare elasticity of mind could have enabled them to fight free from the influence of things once seen and deeds once accomplished. Everything, on the contrary, conspired to make them think that they need only avoid the mistakes which had so nearly lost the last war to win the next one; that they had merely to repeat the methods which, when first tried out, had brought success. I remember writing to a friend, some time in February, as follows: 'One thing is certain: if the High Command makes mistakes this time, they will not be the same mistakes as were made in the Champagne offensive or the Nivelles attack.' Alas! the field of possible mistakes is limitless. What, yesterday, was wisdom may become, to-morrow, the worst of follies.

Doubtless the magic of the past would have had far less power over brains less stiffened by age. It was borne in on me, ever more and more clearly as the campaign developed, that the younger staff officers, most of whom had not served in the earlier war, almost always saw things more clearly than their seniors. Those, it is true, who had been *too* brilliant as pupils remained obstinately loyal to what they had been taught, and they, unfortunately, were the men who filled the most important posts. There were not a few, on the contrary, who had formerly sworn by the words of the master, but now showed an increasing tendency to throw off the intellectual shackles of an education which they were beginning to judge with severity. Even among the mature, but by no means elderly, officers who *had* fought in

1914 or in 1918, there were some who were still capable of absorbing new ideas. But they counted for little. The High Command was dominated by old men.

The methods of promotion followed in peace-time, which make men battalion-commanders at forty, had given us generals of sixty. As frequently happens, these ancient fossils, loaded with honours and sometimes trailing clouds of former glory, quite forgot that in those happy days of achievement they had been young. Consequently, their chief concern was to bar their juniors from the broad road to advancement. Insufficient public attention has been given, on the whole, to the law which, shortly before the outbreak of the present war, created two new grades in the military hierarchy. For a long time there was no higher rank than that of General of Division. It was left to G.H.Q. to determine what function officers holding that rank should perform, and they might just as likely be appointed to the command of an army, or even to that of all the armies, as to a corps, or, still more logically, a division. There can, however, be no real paradise without a pyramid of steps about the celestial throne. So, one fine day it was decided that the posts of Corps or Army Generals, formerly mere functions, should carry with them a definite rank. This, it may be said, was a harmless sop to the vanity of a few men who were rather childishly hungry for distinctions. Actually, it was far from harmless, because once the question of rank comes into the picture, it follows as a matter of discipline that active command shall go to the senior soldier. It became, henceforward, impossible for a young divisional commander, say, to be given an army, unless he had been first promoted to the rank, at the very least, of General of a Corps, because, once in charge of his new formation, he would, by definition, have under him men who already held that grade. Now, the movement from one grade to another is controlled by rules, or at least by usages, which make it much more difficult for an officer to be promoted than merely to be given a new appointment. The members of the War Council, raised, all of them, by the very reform which, doubtless, they had themselves initiated, to the new dignity of Generals of Armies, could therefore hope to keep in their own hands, no matter what might happen, the leadership of the Nation in Arms. Had this system been in operation during the last war, it is extremely improbable that we should ever have seen a young lieutenant-colonel of 1914, called Debeney, leading the First Army in 1918 to the victories of Montdidier and Saint-Quentin, or Colonel Pétain—the Pétain of our youth—flaming through the hierarchy like a prairie-fire, until he reached the topmost pinnacle of all, and ended, one fine summer morning, by marching under the Arc de Triomphe at the head of all the soldiers of France.

When, therefore, after the first setbacks, murmurs began to get around that perhaps the High Command was not wholly blameless, to whom did the Army turn in its search for young blood and energetic leadership? The Chief of Staff of one of the generalissimos of the former war was made Commander-in-Chief, while another of those generalissimos was appointed as his technical adviser. The first of these gentlemen had held the post of Vice-President of the War Council, the second, at about the same time, had been Minister for War. In other words, both of them had been in some degree responsible for the very methods which had just been proved to be so shatteringly inadequate.

So completely dominated were our military, and even our civil, governors by the superstition of age, and by the respect due to a prestige which, though certainly venerable, ought, if only for its own self-protection, to have been laid in the purple shroud befitting dead gods, that they became the victims of a false cult, and bowed in homage to an incarnation of experience which, just because it drew its so-called lessons from the past, was almost bound to misinterpret the present. True, one of the more recently promoted Generals of Brigade was called in to advise the Government, but what did he do? I do not actually know, but I very much fear that among the glorious constellations of that much-studded sky, his two poor little stars did not shine very brightly. The Committee of Public Safety would have made him Commander-in-Chief. As it was, our war, up to the very end, was a war of old men, or of theorists who were bogged down in errors engendered by the faulty teaching of history. It was saturated by the smell of decay rising from the Staff College, the offices of a peace-time General Staff, and the barrack-square. The world belongs to those who are in love with the new. That is why our High Command, finding itself face to face with novelty, and being quite incapable of seizing its opportunities, not only experienced defeat, but, like boxers who have run to fat and are thrown off their balance by the first unexpected blow, accepted it.

But our leaders would not have succumbed so easily to that spirit of apathy which wise theologians have ever held to be among the worst of sins, had they merely entertained doubts of their own competence. In their hearts, they were only too ready to despair of the country they had been called upon to defend, and of the people who furnished the soldiers they commanded.

At this point I leave the purely military field. The roots of a misunderstanding so grave that we cannot but rank it among the main causes of our disaster, must be sought elsewhere and at a much deeper level.

Chapter Three

A FRENCHMAN EXAMINES HIS
CONSCIENCE

IN no nation is any professional group ever entirely responsible for its own actions. The solidarity of society as a whole is too strong to permit the existence of the sort of moral autonomy, existing in isolation, which any such total responsibility would seem to imply. The staffs worked with tools which were put into their hands by the nation at large. The psychological conditions in which they lived were not altogether of their own making, and they themselves, through their members, were as their origins had moulded them. They could be only what the totality of the social *fact*, as it existed in France, permitted them to be. That is why I cannot rest content with what I have so far written. I trust that I am honest: certainly, I have done my best to describe, in the terms of my own experience, what I believe to have been the vices of our military system, and the part played by them in the defeat of my country. But, unless I am to be guilty of betraying a trust, I must go farther. The very nature of my inquiry makes it necessary that the evidence of the soldier be balanced and completed by the self-examination of the Frenchman.

I do not joyfully or lightly embark on this part of my task. As a Frenchman I feel constrained, in speaking of my country, to say of her only what is good. It is a harsh duty that compels a man to make a public show of his mother's weaknesses when she is in misery and despair. As an historian, I know better than do most men how difficult it is to conduct an analysis which, if it is to have any value, must be concerned with a complex of causes, remote, involved, and, in the present state of sociological science, extremely difficult to uncover. But personal scruples are, in this matter, wholly unimportant. My children, when they read this balance-sheet of history, the unknown friends into whose hands it may some day come, must not be allowed to reproach its author with having played tricks with truth, of having condemned a number of glaring faults, while, at the same time, maintaining a deliberate silence about errors for which every citizen was, in part, responsible.

The men at the front are rarely satisfied with their companions in the rear. It needs an unusually large dose of generosity, when one is sleeping on the hard ground, to forgive old friends the comfort of their beds, or, when machine-guns are rat-tatting over one's head, to think without bitterness of the prosperous security of shops still crammed with customers and the peaceful delights of provincial cafés to the habitués of which war means no more than leisurely discussions of points of strategical theory. It is when battle ends in disaster that the gulf separating these two halves of the nation threatens to become permanent. The soldier is only too conscious of the sacrifices he has been called upon to make. If they turn out to have been useless, that, he feels, is not *his* responsibility. His leaders, ever fearful of his criticism, encourage him to find scapegoats anywhere rather than in the Army. Thus is born the fatal legend of the 'stab in the back' which reactionary movements and military *coups d'état* always find so useful. I hope that in what I have so far written I have made it clear that some, at least, of the veterans of 1940 will refuse to listen to such sowers of discord. But it is no use pretending that the back areas were not, to some extent, as deserving of blame as the armies.

But were there, could there, in fact, be any back areas, using that term in the sense which is normally attached to it? France in arms between the years 1915 and 1918 was composed of several *slices* of territory arranged in depth. On the map of danger each was coloured differently. First came the scorched zone of the front line. It did not, of course, remain static, but any withdrawal which might take it, say, from the outskirts of Saint-Quentin to the suburbs of Noyon, seemed to us a pretty serious matter. Yet in mere distance the area of retreat meant no more than half an hour's run by car. Slightly farther back was the 'advanced rear', a thinnish strip in which lay our rest billets, still relatively exposed to attack. Last of all came the *real* rear, stretching to infinity: a place of quiet towns and unravaged fields. Now and again, to be sure, some sudden alarm—usually regarded as providing a mild cause of scandal—might, for a moment or two, trouble the peace of this happy refuge. A Junker might fly over Paris, a Zeppelin might drop a few bombs, Big Bertha might unexpectedly hit the ornamental water in a public park, or, with more tragic success, the pillars of a church. Crouching in the trenches we trembled for the safety of our families. But what were such trivial occurrences compared with our more recent memories?

For air bombardment and the speed of modern war have completely disarranged our pattern of familiar dangers. No stretch of sky is nowadays devoid of menace, and motorized elements, against which no fixed 'line' is ever proof, eat up the miles. In the space of a few minutes hundreds of people met their deaths at Rennes, that town of Brittany where, only yesterday, one would have thought oneself to be as safe from war's alarms as in the heart of America. The roads of Berry were swept by machine-gun fire, and the bullets treated soldier and child alike. These things are true enough, but I sometimes wonder whether such horrors are quite the novelty that some suppose. In its power of wreaking concentrated destruction, and, especially, in its speed of movement, the bomber of the skies has, I admit, no precedent in history. But only a relatively short time ago it was the common thing for war to pile up more victims in the stripped and starving fields, in the streets of looted cities, than in the ranks of the actual combatants. Men's memories are short. Such times are real only to a handful of old fogies who live out their lives among the musty tomes of ancient libraries. The average human being finds in the immediate past a convenient screen to set between himself and the distant truths of history. It keeps him from realizing that the embalmed tragedies of an older day may once again become realities. It was only, he thinks, in the Dark Ages that war brought death to any but the fighting men. Quite recently, the civil populations of the back areas, and those whose duties lay in offices and depots, really believed that there was a difference, in terms of danger, between front and rear.

Not but what we had every reason to be sceptical, and I believe that most men, in their secret hearts, were shaken in their comfortable faith. We had been warned. Had not the news-reels shown us terrible pictures of Spain in ruins? Had not correspondent after correspondent told us of the martyrdom suffered by the cities of Poland? In a sense we had been *over-*warned: of that I am convinced. Enemy propaganda was adept in harping on the single string of aerial bombardment. Paris might have been defended; the old superstition about 'open cities' might not, to the extent it did, have hampered operations, if only the fate of Madrid, of Nankin, of Warsaw had not been so vivid in the public eye. We had been told enough about it all to be afraid, but not enough, and not in the right way, to make us accept the inevitable, to make us realize that civilian morale must be adapted to these new, or, rather, to these resuscitated, conditions of war.

I am not, I think, temperamentally insensitive to the claims of pity, though what I saw with my own eyes in two successive wars may have somewhat deadened my responses. But one thing I shall never be able to witness unmoved—the look of terror on the faces of children running in village streets from falling bombs. I pray God that I may never again have to see *that,* whether in reality or in my dreams. It is intolerable that war should involve the very young—not only because in them the hope of the future lies, but because in their weakness and their irresponsibility they make so confident an appeal to our protection. Christian legend would not, I think, have been so hard on Herod if he had been guilty only of the Baptist's death. The crime for which he could never find pardon was the Massacre of the Innocents.

Confronted by the nation's peril and by the duties that it lays on every citizen, all adults are equal, and only a curiously warped mind would claim for any of them the privilege of immunity. What, after all, *is* a 'civilian' in time of war? He is nothing more than a man whose weight of years, whose health, whose profession (if it be judged essential to the well-being of his country) prevents him from bearing arms effectively. To find himself thus kept from serving his fellows in the one way that any citizen would wish to do is a misfortune for any man. Why should it confer on him the right to escape from the common danger? In a few years from now I shall be too old for mobilization. My sons will take my place. Am I, therefore, to conclude that my life has become more precious than theirs? Far better, on the contrary, that their youth should be preserved, if necessary, at the cost of my grey hairs. Herodotus said, a long time ago, that the great impiety of war is that it forces fathers to consign their children to the tomb. Should it be a matter of complaint for us that Nature's law has once more come into its own? For the nation at large there can be no worse tragedy than having to sacrifice those very lives on which her destiny reposes. Against the strength of those young bodies we others weigh but lightly in the scale. Nor do I except the women, save only those young mothers whose survival is necessary in the interests of their children. Girls to-day laugh at the swooning habits of their grandmothers. They are right to do so, and I am certain that courage in them is no less natural than in us, nor less a duty. In the days of professional armies the soldier, whether knight or mercenary, shed his blood for his patron, and for this service the non-combatants paid in rents and wages. If he put their safety in peril they had a just ground of complaint, for the contract had been broken. To-day, when every fit man is a soldier, no one in the menaced city can escape the tedium and the risks. To share them is his bounden duty. To maintain otherwise is mere sentimentality—or cowardice.

These self-evident truths are so simple that one feels a certain shame at having to call men's attention to them. But were they generally understood in the course of those months through which we lived but recently? I find it hard to believe. Too many mayors thought it their duty to ask that their towns should not be defended; too many leaders, military as well as civilian, were only too willing to act in accordance with this fallacious conception of the public interest. Truth to tell, such timid souls were not moved solely by the wish—in itself admirable—to save human lives. The fearful destruction of property that had accompanied the war of 1914–18 left bitter memories. Everybody knew that the artistic heritage of the country had been cruelly mutilated, and our national prosperity to a large extent compromised. There was a feeling that it would be better to accept any humiliation rather than undergo a second time this twin impoverishment. It was a strange form of wisdom that did not even ask whether, in fact, there could be any worse catastrophe, for our culture or for the system of our economic life, than to let ourselves be conquered by a robber society.

A day came when the decision was taken to declare all cities of more than 20,000 inhabitants 'open'. That a village lived in by poor yokels should be bombed, smashed, and burned was, apparently, a matter of indifference to the noble apostles of humanity who upheld this view. But a city of solid tradesmen was quite another matter! ... And so it came about that while the cadets of Saumur were being killed on the Loire, the enemy had already cut the bridges behind them at Nantes, because these were regarded as being 'out of bounds'. It is no good mincing words. This timidity of the nation at large was, no doubt, in many cases but the sum of the timidity of individuals. There were cases of officials leaving their posts without orders. Many instructions to evacuate were issued before they need have been. A sort of frenzy of flight swept over the whole country. It was no rare thing, along the roads crowded with refugees, to come on complete local fire-brigades perched on their engines. At the first rumour of the enemy's advance, off they had rushed to find safety for their persons and their property. I am convinced that they had been *told* to do so. Their towns could perish in the flames, provided the means of mastering the blaze could be got out of the danger-zone. . . . Such, it will be said, are ever the charming ways of bureaucracy. Alas! the evil went a great deal deeper than that. I know of at least one industrial centre where, on the approach of the German columns, the managers hastily abandoned the factories without even bothering to see that their workpeople were paid. Had they been called up for service in one of the armed services, they would probably have stuck gamely to their posts. But they were 'civilians', and, as such, they forgot, or had not been sufficiently reminded, that in time of war private professional interests no longer exist. When the nation is in arms, only one thing matters—the fighting front.

Am I wrong? Am I, too, guilty of yielding to that fond temptation of the old who, remembering the days of their youth, too readily underestimate their juniors? I have a feeling that, even among the men of military age, something had been lost of that fervent fraternity in danger which meant so much to most of us in the old 1914 days. There can be little doubt that people had grown to regard certain causes of 'exemption' not as tiresome and rather humiliating necessities, but as privileges, almost as 'rights'. Too often the word had gone out to workers on the land, 'Why should factory hands get out of it, and not you?'; to fathers of families, 'Your first concern is your duty to your children'; to veterans of the last war, 'Twice in a lifetime is really *too* much!' When the Ministry of Munitions was re-organized and expanded, the spectacle of a lot of reserve officers pelting along as hard as they could go for the comfortable security of its office chairs made us feel slightly sick. Off they went, crying as they took their leave of us, 'It really is an awful bore, but it seems they can't do without us!' Were they, all of them, *quite* so indispensable? Could not they, sometimes at least, have been replaced by older men? I frequently heard well-meaning persons express the hope that at least our young intel-lectuals should this time be spared the sacrifices which had decimated their ranks during the last war. In my ears, I must confess, this sentiment had a false ring. It was terrible, no doubt, that so many young hopefuls should have perished on the Marne, the Yser, and the Somme. The wound thus given to the intel-lectual life of the nation has never ceased to bleed. But, once the issue of arms had been joined, was there nothing to be set in the opposite balance? Surely, nothing could have been worse for intellectual freedom, for national culture, for moral health, than defeat? When sacrifice is the order of the day, any exception should be out of the question. No one is justified in regarding his own life as of more value than the lives of his neighbours. Once that sort of doubt is allowed to creep in, each one of us, in his own sphere, whether it be great or small, can always find perfectly legitimate reasons for regarding himself as 'indis-pensable'.

I do not know what part this desire to spare the young may have played in the curious reluctance of the authorities to raise and train recruits. At the moment of the final catastrophe most of the 1940 class had only just been called up. They had, for practical purposes, received no useful instruction of any kind. In most of the big cities no attempt had been made to provide preliminary training for the younger boys, many of whom asked for nothing better than to be allowed to follow in the footsteps of their elders. Where did the responsibility for this incredible negligence lie?—with the High Command or with the Civil Government? (But, surely, if the soldiers had insisted, they could have got their way?) I do not know what the motives were that underlay this decision. Are we really to believe that the interminable period of waiting, with its almost negligible losses, had rendered our leaders forgetful of the need to have ready trained the reserves on whom they would have to count once the real fighting had begun? If that is so, then it was not the least disastrous of the many results of that 'bogged-down' period of the war—as the Germans called it—which we had so foolishly welcomed at the time. 'The real trouble is, we've got too *many* men' said an officer to one of my friends who, when he was sent home on the grounds that he had got a growing family, had asked to be allowed to remain with the colours. Was it feared that we should not have sufficient equipment?—or was it that, haunted by the memory of that unfortunate class of 1916 which we had seen, with tears in our eyes, flung into the furnace of the Somme almost straight from school, the authorities had—as I thought at the time—yielded to the claims of a somewhat excessive sentimentality? Whatever the reasons, there can be no doubt that our governors, both individually and as a class, did lack something of that ruthless heroism which becomes so necessary when the country is in danger.

But this very question of the 'governing class' raises questions which need very careful consideration. In the France of 1939 the members of the upper middle class were never sick of declaring that they had lost all power. This was an exaggeration. Solidly supported by the banks and the Press, the régime of the *élite* was not, to that extent, 'finished'. But it *is* true that the great industrialists no longer held a monopoly in the running of the country. The leaders of the principal trade unions, and, to a smaller extent, the mass of the wage-earners, had risen to a position of power in the affairs of the Republic. That had been obvious in 1938, when a certain minister—a 'Man of Munich' if ever there was one—used them as intermediaries when he set about spreading an atmosphere of panic in order to cover up his own weakness. There can be no denying that if much heavy responsibility in this war rested on the shoulders of the military authorities, a considerable amount of blame must also be laid at the door of the trade unions.

I am about to speak of matters of which I have no first-hand knowledge. I need hardly stress the fact that the life of the factory, both before and during the period of hostilities, lay far outside my normal field of operations. But the evidence which I have amassed is so unanimous, and comes from so many different sources, ranging in variety from chief engineers to machine-minders, that I am forced to accept its conclusions as valid. The output of our war factories was insufficient. We were not turning out enough aeroplanes, engines, or tanks. I do not for a moment believe that it was only, or even principally, the wage-earners who were to blame for this state of affairs. On the other hand, it would ill become them to plead complete innocence. Forgetful of the fact that they too, in their own way, were just as much soldiers as the men in uniform, they thought first and foremost about selling their labour at the highest price: in other words, about doing as little as possible, for the shortest time possible, in return for as much money as possible. In normal times that would be a perfectly natural attitude. 'Sordid materialism!' once exclaimed a certain politician whose own enthusiasm for the spiritual was not, I should have said, particularly obvious. But that, of course, is sheer nonsense. The manual worker is out to sell the strength of his arms. The men who sell textiles, sugar, or armaments are scarcely in a position to be shocked if he applies to his own case the great law of trade, which is to give little and to receive much. But however legitimate that point of view may be at other times, it is cruelly out of place when the very existence of one's country is at stake, and when those at the front are risking their lives. The plumber of the village where I live told me that when he was called up to work in a war factory the other men used to hide his tools to prevent him from turning out more, or working more quickly, than was permitted by the unwritten 'law' of the shop. That is an undeniable fact, and it provides a terrible indictment. But to suppose for a moment that that kind of indifference to the interests of the nation was general in one whole class of the population would be the height of injustice. I am more than ready to admit that there were honourable exceptions. Still, this attitude was quite widely enough spread for its consequences to weigh heavily in the scales of war. How it arose at all needs to be explained.

It has been said again and again, and by all sorts of people, that this war failed to rouse the deepest feelings of the nation to a much larger extent than did the last one. I believe that view to be entirely wrong. Our people are temperamentally disinclined actively to *want* any war. No Frenchman in 1939 burned with the desire to 'die for Danzig'. But then it is equally true to say that in 1914 none of them was particularly anxious to 'die for Belgrade'. The *camarilla* which hatched its plots around the Serbian throne was no more familiar to our workers and peasants than was, twenty years later, the corrupt government of Polish colonels; nor if it had been would it have fanned them to a white heat of enthusiasm. As to Alsace-Lorraine, though it is, no doubt, true that when the actual fighting began in 1914, a picture of the martyred provinces did suddenly emerge in men's minds from that decent obscurity which, only a few days earlier, had still shrouded it, but that was merely under the pressure of a necessity which, for quite other reasons, had already been accepted by the nation. Since we had been forced to take up arms, it was difficult to imagine that we should lay them down before we had delivered our lost brothers. Certainly, the beautiful Alsatian eyes, which the popular prints of the time were so fond of depicting, would never, of themselves, have had sufficient influence, in peace-time, on a public opinion which was concerned only to maintain the security of the nation's homes; would never have persuaded men lightly to launch their country on an adventure bristling with the most appalling dangers, with the sole object of drying those bewitching tears.

The truth of the matter is that on both occasions the national response drew its vigour from the same source. '*They're* always picking a quarrel with the rest of the world. The more we give 'em, the more they'll want. It just can't go on like this.' That was what one of my neighbours in a little village of the Creuse said to me shortly before I left for Strasbourg. A peasant of 1914 would have expressed himself in much the same words. As a matter of fact, if either of the two wars was more likely than the other to appeal to the deepest instincts of the masses, and especially of the industrial masses, it was undoubtedly the second, and that because of the very 'ideological' complexion which so many have blamed, but which did succeed in giving a touch of beauty to the sacrifices entailed. The men of the factories and the fields would no more, in 1939, have *deliberately* shed their blood for the overthrow of the dictators than would their elders of 1914 for the liberation of Alsace-Lorraine. But once the battle had been joined against those same dictators, and as a result of *their* action, they felt that by fighting they were helping forward one of the great tasks of humanity. To believe otherwise is to show complete ignorance of the high nobility which lies unexpressed in the hearts of a people which, like ours, has behind it a long history of political action. The absurd ineptitude of our official propaganda, its irritating and crude optimism, its timidity, and, above all, the inability of our rulers to give a frank definition of their war aims, may well, during the long months of inaction, have muddied to some extent what, in the early days, had been so crystal-clear. In May 1940 the spirit that had animated the men when they were first mobilized was not yet dead. Those for whom the *Marseillaise* was still a rallying-song had not ceased to link it with the cult of patriotism and the hatred of tyrants.

The trouble was that among the wage-earners these instincts, which were still strong, and which a less pusillanimous government would have known how to encourage, were at variance with certain other, and more recent, tendencies which were at work within the collective mind. I, with most of the men of my generation, had built enormous hopes, when we were young, on the trade-union movement. But we made no allowance for the narrowness of outlook which, little by little, choked the enthusiasm of the early, epic struggles. What was the cause of this failure? Partly, no doubt, an inevitable preoccupation with wage-claims, and a consequent scaling-down of interest and policy; partly, too, the fact that Labour's leaders allowed themselves to get tangled up in the old political game of electoral propaganda and lobbying. However that may be, it is true to say that the trade-union movement has shown a growing tendency everywhere to diverge from the road on which its feet were originally set, as though dogged by some ineluctable Fate.

Everyone knows that word *kleinbürgerlich* with which Marx stigmatized all politico-social movements which confined themselves to the narrow field of partial interests. Could anything have been more *kleinbürgerlich*, more *petit bourgeois*, than the attitude adopted in the last few years, and even during the war, by most of the big unions, and especially by those which included civil servants in their ranks? I have attended not a few meetings of my own professional organization. Its members were drawn from the intellectual class, but it is true to say that scarcely ever did they show real concern for anything except—not money on a large scale, but what I may call the small change of remuneration. They seemed to be blissfully unaware of such problems as the rôle which our corporation might play in the life of the country; nor were they ever prepared to discuss the bigger question of France's material future. Their vision was limited to immediate issues of petty profit, and I am afraid that this blindness marked the conduct of most of the big unions. I saw something of the way in which the Post Office workers and the railwaymen behaved both during and after the war, and the spectacle was not a very edifying one. Most of them, I am sure, were very decent fellows; a few, as events showed, could on occasion conduct themselves like heroes. But is it by any means certain that the rank and file, and, what is more important, their representatives, ever really understood that the days through which we were living called for more than parish-pump politics? Did they, I mean, fully realize what was demanded of them in pursuance of their daily work? That, after all, is the touchstone of the professional conscience. In most of the cities of western France during the month of June I saw hordes of wretched men wandering about the streets in an effort to get back to their homes. All of them were carrying loads far heavier than they could cope with, and why? Simply because the railway stations had seen fit to close their left-luggage offices for fear of imposing on their staffs a few hours of overtime, or of rather heavier work than usual. It was this kind of short-sightedness, this kind of administrative bumbledom, the effect of petty rivalry and a refusal to get the last ounce out of their members—so different from the dynamic energy of a Pelloutier[1]—which explains the nervelessness of the trade-union movement all over Europe, and not least in France, when confronted by the first aggressive moves of the dictator states. It accounts for their war record. What did a few noisy 'resolutions', aimed at the gallery, matter? The point is that the general run of organized labour never got it into their heads that the only thing that counted was as complete and as rapid a victory as possible for their country, and the defeat, not only of Nazism, but of all those elements of its philo-

[1] Fernand Pelloutier was a militant trade-union leader in the period 1914-18, and played an active part in the administration of the C.G.T.

sophy which its imitators, in the event of success, would inevitably borrow. They had not been taught, as they should have been by leaders worthy of the name, to look above, beyond, and around the petty problems of every day. By concentrating attention on matters concerned with the earning of their daily bread, they ran the risk of discovering that there might be no daily bread to earn. And now the hour of doom has sounded. Seldom has short-sightedness been more harshly punished.

Then, too, there was the ideology of international pacifism. I flatter myself that I am a good citizen of the world, and among the least chauvinistic of men. As an historian, I know that there is a good deal of truth in Karl Marx's slogan of 'Workers of the World Unite!' I have seen too much of war not to know that it is both horrible and senseless. But the narrowness of outlook which I have just been denouncing consists precisely in a refusal to bring these sentiments into harmonious relation with other forms of enthusiasm which are no less worthy of respect. I have never believed that because a man loves his country he cannot also love his children, nor can I see why any form of internationalism, whether of the intellect or of class interests, should be irreconcilable with patriotism. I go farther, and say, after carefully searching my own conscience, that this presumed antinomy has no real existence at all. It is a poor heart that cannot find room for more than one kind of affection.

But let us not linger in this world of the emotions. Those of us who have a certain degree of self-respect, who hate big words which have become so popularly debased that they no longer express the intimate truths of mind and heart, find it difficult to breathe its atmosphere for long without a sensation of nausea. Besides, that particular world is one into which the pacifists did not as a rule ask us to follow them. What they primarily invoked was the sentiment of self-interest; and it was because they made of this presumed self-interest an image woefully at variance with any true knowledge of their fellow men, that they overweighted with error the minds of the somewhat sheep-like disciples who trusted them. They said that French capitalism was a hard task-master; and in that they were certainly not wrong. But what they forgot was that victory for the authoritarian régimes would be bound to lead to the complete enslavement of the workers. Were they really blind to the fact that the profiteers-to-be of our defeat were already on the prowl ready to seize upon it—nay, actually hoping that it would occur? They taught, not without reason, that war builds up a mass of useless destruction. But they omitted to distinguish between a war which men have deliberately planned, and a war imposed from without; between murder and legitimate self-defence. To those who asked them whether they did not think it was one's duty to wring the neck of the execu-tioner, they replied: 'No one's attacking us'—for they loved to play with words. Maybe, having lost the habit of looking their own thoughts fairly and squarely in the face, they had allowed themselves to be caught in the tangle of their own equivocations. The highwayman does not say to his victim, 'It's your blood I'm after'; he offers him a choice—'Your money or your life'. Similarly, when an aggressor nation sets out to oppress its neighbours it says: 'Either abdicate your liberty or take the consequence of massacre.' They maintained that war is the concern of the rich and powerful, that the poor should have nothing to do with it. As though, in an old society, cemented by centuries of a shared culture, the humble are not always, for good or ill, constrained to make common cause with the mighty. They whispered—I have heard them—that Hitler was not nearly so black as he was painted; that the nation would save itself a great deal of suffering by opening its gates to the enemy, instead of setting itself to oppose invasion by force of arms. How, I wonder, do these noble apostles feel to-day in that occupied zone which lies in starvation beneath the jack-boot of tyranny?

Since the gospel they preached was one of seeming con-venience, their sermons found an easy echo in those lazy, selfish instincts which exist in all men's hearts side by side with nobler potentialities. These enthusiasts, many of whom were not, as individuals, lacking in courage, worked unconsciously to produce a race of cowards. For it is an undoubted truth that unless virtue is accompanied by severe self-criticism, it always runs the risk of turning against its own most dearly held convictions. Dear fellow teachers—when it came to the point, you did, for the most part, put up a magnificent fight. It was your goodwill which managed to create in many a sleepy secondary school, in many a tradition-ridden university, the only form of education of which, perhaps, we can feel genuinely proud. I only hope that a day will come, and come soon, a day of glory and of happiness for France, when, liberated from the enemy, and freer than ever in our intellectual life, we may meet again for the mutual discussion of ideas. And when that happens, do you not think that, having learned from an experience so dearly purchased, you will find much to alter in the things you were teaching only a few years back?

But what is really remarkable is that these extremist lovers of the human race showed no surprise at all when, on the road that led to capitulation, they found themselves walking arm in arm with the born enemies of their class, the sworn foes of their ideals. As a matter of fact, odd though such an alliance may seem, its intellectual basis is to be found in conditions long antecedent to a supervening political hostility. Among those with whom they had more than once crossed swords on the battlefield of the hustings, with whom now they were prepared to collaborate in the work of securing peace at any price, were many who had the same social background as themselves, though they had taken early flight to richer feeding-grounds. These turncoats had long hidden away all that might remind people of their earlier enthusiasm for revolution. Old clothes of just that cut, they thought, might prove a shade embarrassing in the circumstances of their new lives. But, in their onward march, they had passed through many political parties, and something of what they had found there had remained indelibly impressed upon them. They had lost all sense of national values, and were quite incapable of finding them again. It is no accident that the collapse of our country brought to power a minister who was once at Kienthal,[1] nor will it be one if the Germans, wishing to elevate to a position of influence some gutter-agitator, should pick on a man who, before assuming in the years before the war a wash of sham patriotism, had been a Communist leader. Against one particular school of politics no more terrible charge can be brought than this: that once a man has been formed by it, he may forget everything it taught him, including much that was fine, much that was noble, save only this—the denial of his country.

Thus it came about that though the general needs of our national defence were more inextricably than ever bound up with the interests of the wage-earners, they made demands upon the working class which, however legitimately obvious they may have been, were compromised by a spirit of uncertainty and gloom in the factories. This vague lack of purpose was bad enough: it was made far worse by the incredible contradictions of French Communism.

But here I find myself coming to grips with an entirely different order of problems which belong, strictly, to the world of thought.

It was not only in the field that intellectual causes lay at the root of our defeat. As a nation we had been content with incomplete knowledge and imperfectly thought-out ideas. Such an attitude is not a good preparation for military success. Our system of government demands the participation of the masses. The destiny of the People is in their own hands, and I see no

[1] Kienthal is the name of the small Swiss town where, during the First World War (in 1916), Pierre Laval met a number of Swiss and German representatives and discussed with them the possibility of reaching a 'Peace by Agreement'. After 1940 the expression 'a man of Kienthal' was used to describe anyone who sought peace at any price—even at the price of national dishonour.

reason for believing that they are not perfectly capable of choosing rightly. But what effort had been made to supply them with that minimum of clear and definite information without which no rational conduct is possible? To that question the answer is 'None'. In no way did our so-called democratic system so signally fail. That particular dereliction of duty constituted the most heinous crime of our self-styled democrats. The matter would be less serious if what we had to deplore were merely the lies and half-truths inspired by party loyalties openly avowed. Wicked these may be, but, on the whole, they can be fairly easily discounted. Far graver is the fact that our national Press, claiming to provide an impartial news-service, was sailing under false colours. Many newspapers, even those which openly wore the livery of party beliefs, were secretly enslaved to unavowed and, often, squalid interests. Some of them were controlled by foreign influences. I do not deny that the common sense of the ordinary reader did, to some extent, counterbalance this, but only at the cost of developing an attitude of scepticism to *all* propaganda, printed and broadcast alike. It would be a great mistake to think that the elector always votes as 'his' paper tells him to. I have known more than one humble citizen who votes almost automatically *against* the views expressed by his chosen rag, and it may be that this refusal to be stampeded by printed insincerities is among the more consoling elements of our contemporary national life. It does, at least, offer some hope for the future. Still, it must be admitted that such an attitude provides a poor intellectual training for those who are called upon to understand what is at stake in a vast world struggle, to judge rightly of the coming storm, and to arm themselves adequately against its violence. Quite deliberately—as one can see by reading *Mein Kampf* or the records of Rauschning's conversations—Hitler kept the truth from his servile masses. Instead of intellectual persuasion he gave them emotional suggestion. For us there is but one set of alternatives. Either, like the Germans, we must turn our people into a keyboard on which a few leaders can play at will (but who are those leaders? The playing of those at present on the stage is curiously lacking in resonance); or we can so train them that they may be able to collaborate to the full with the representatives in whose hands they have placed the reins of government. At the present stage of civilization this dilemma admits of no middle term. . . . The masses no longer obey. They *follow*, either because they have been hypnotized or because they *know*.

Is it true to say that our comfortable and relatively educated classes thought it wiser—from motives of contempt or mistrust —*not* to keep the man in the street, or in the fields, accurately informed? That some such feeling did exist there can be small doubt. It was traditional. The European *bourgeoisie* had never been really happy about letting the 'lower classes' learn to read. An historian could quote many texts bearing on this point. But the evil had gone much deeper. Even those who were in a position to satisfy their curiosity lacked the desire to do so. Compare two newspapers which carry almost precisely the same title: *The Times* and *Le Temps*. Both are controlled by roughly similar interests; both appeal to a public which is far removed from the level of the herd; the impartiality of both is equally suspect. Still, allowing for all that, the reader of the first will be infinitely better informed about the world as it is than the regular subscriber to the second. The same contrast is to be found if one compares those organs of the French Press which take most pride in what they call their 'good manners', with, say, the *Frankfurter Zeitung*—not only with the *Frankfurter* of pre-Hitlerian days, but even with its modern successor. The wise man, says the proverb, is contented with little. In the field of information, our middle class has certainly been, in the sense intended by the sober Epicurus, terribly wise.

This symptom is confirmed by a hundred others. In the course of two wars I rubbed shoulders with a large number of officers, regulars and reservists alike, who varied very considerably in their social origins. Among those who did even a little reading (and they were pretty thin on the ground) I scarcely ever saw one with a book in his hands which might have helped him to a better understanding of the present by shedding on it the light of the past. The only copy at 'Q' of Strasser's book on Hitler was brought there by me. Only one of my colleagues ever asked to borrow it. The poverty of our municipal libraries has often been made a matter of scandal. Look at the public balance-sheet of any of our city administrations, and you will admit that 'indigence' is the better word. About 1 November 1918—long before Germany had started burning books—I had occasion to visit, at Vouziers, a 'field library' which had been abandoned by the retreating enemy. Its contents were far from being confined to thrillers or political tracts. Have *we* ever tried to provide our troops with anything comparable? It is not only to the art of knowing others that we have allowed ourselves to become strangers. What have we done about the old maxim which says 'Know thyself'? I have been told that on one of the International Commissions our delegate was publicly laughed at by his Polish colleague because, of all the nations represented, we alone were unable to provide a serious statistical table of wage-rates. The heads of our great industrial undertakings have always pinned their faith to secrecy—which favours the petty interests of individual—rather than to that knowledge openly displayed which assists collective action. In this century of chemists they have retained the mental outlook of alchemists. Study, for a moment, the behaviour of those groups whose self-imposed task it formerly was to combat the spread of Communism. It should have been obvious that only an honest inquiry, intelligently conducted, up and down the country, stood any chance of providing reliable information about the causes of a success which was giving them such a headache, and of doing something, perhaps, to arrest its progress. But none of the individuals con-

146

cerned ever thought of such a thing. The political motive which lay behind this particular activity is not, here, my concern. The point I want to make is that, whether one be sympathetic or hostile to what was proposed, the intellectual efficiency of this powerful association of interests was hopelessly inadequate. Is it to be wondered at that our military staffs organized their Intelligence Services so badly? Their members belonged to a social class in which the taste for self-education was suffering from creeping paralysis. They were the kind of men who could read *Mein Kampf* and still entertain doubts about the true intentions of the Nazi policy. Because they have little 'realistic' curiosity, and are proud of it, they would seem to doubt them even to-day.

But the worst of this mental laziness is that, almost inevitably, it leads to a sort of gloomy mood of self-satisfaction. Every day I hear 'back to the land' sermons on the radio. The French people, maimed and abandoned, are told: 'You let yourselves be deluded by the charms of a far too highly mechanized civilization. By accepting its laws and its products, you turned away from those ancient values which made you what you are. You had become chaff of the great city, of the factory, perhaps, even, of the school, whereas what your nature craves is the village or the market-town familiar to your ancestors, the primitive farming methods of ancient days, the small, compact society governed by its local notables. Those are the waters in which you must bathe if you are to recover your former greatness.' I am well aware that under these fine words there lay concealed— and not so very successfully concealed either—interests which have nothing whatever to do with the happiness and prosperity of France. A great many people who sit in the driver's seat to-day—or think they do—have never ceased to regret the docility which they believe to be inherent in all mildly successful peasant societies (not that they are right. Our country folk have always had what the old chroniclers call *la nuque dure*—have always, in other words, been 'pretty tough'). But it is chiefly Germany, now that she has triumphed by the machine, who wants to hold the monopoly of machine methods. She wants to surround herself with humble vassal nations, and these have got to be purely agricultural societies which can be compelled, in the years to come, to exchange, at prices fixed by the conqueror, their corn and their dairy produce for the output of her heavy industries. The voice on the radio may speak our language, but it comes from the other side of the Rhine. These bucolic recommendations are, however, nothing new. They were made familiar to us, in the years before the war, through a whole literature of renunciation. It was for ever, this literature, lashing what it called 'Americanization'. It denounced the dangers of the machine and of material progress. It contrasted these things, to their disadvantage, with the quiet pleasures of the country-side, with the grace of a civilization dominated by the small market-town, with the charm, as well as with the hidden strength, of a society which it called upon to remain increasingly loyal to the ways of life of a vanished age. The theme was purely academic, or, it would be truer to say, childish. Our older authors of the country-side, men like Noël du Fail and Olivier de Serres, would have laughed it out of court. There is more of endurance than of charm about genuine rural labour, and it is only in the *Eclogues* that the village appears as an abode of peace. Not that there was not a certain amount of truth in the glorification of country ways. I am convinced that even to-day a people can gain much from having its life rooted in the soil, for only thus will it give to its economic development a solidity which is rare in the modern world, and ensure the existence of those reserves of human vitality which nothing else can replace. From having seen at first hand how he lives, from having once fought at his side, and from having much pondered the details of his history, I know the true worth of the French peasant, the vigour and the unwearied quickness of his mind. I can feel as vividly as anybody else the modest charm of our old market-towns, and I am well aware that they served as the mould in which, through long ages, was formed all that is most active in the French character.

But are we prepared to be what the Italians have declared that they will never consent to be, a mere 'historical museum'? It is no use pretending: the choice is not really open to us. Even if it were, we know only too well the fate reserved by our enemies for museums. We want to live, and if we are to live we must emerge from this struggle victorious. Let us at least have the courage to admit that what so far has been conquered in our land is precisely the life of our dear, dead towns. The leisurely rhythm of their days, their crawling motor-buses, their sleepy officials, the time lost in their soft atmosphere of lethargy, the lazy ease of their café-life, their local politics and petty trades, their empty libraries, their taste for the past, and their mistrust of anything that may shake them out of their comfortable habits. These are the things that have succumbed before the hellish onset of that 'dynamic' Germany whose aggression was backed by the resources of a national life organized on the principle of the hive. If only to preserve what can, and ought to, be of value in our great heritage, we must adapt ourselves to the claims of a new age. The donkey-cart may be a friendly and a charming means of transport, but if we refuse to replace it by the motor-car, where the motor-car is desirable, we shall find ourselves stripped of everything—including the donkey. But if we are to set about building the new, we must first acquire the necessary knowledge. If our officers failed to master the methods of warfare imposed upon them by the contemporary world, that was largely because, in the contemporary world, our middle classes, from which they were drawn, had been willing to keep their eyes lazily shut to the facts. If we turn back on ourselves we shall be lost. Salvation can be ours only on condition that we set our brains to work with a will, in order that we may *know* more fully, and get our imaginations moving to a quicker tempo.

We must, too, recover that coherence of thought of which, in recent years, a strange sickness seems to have deprived all those in France who have been active in politics, whether on a large or a small scale. No historian is likely to feel much surprise that the 'Right-Wing' parties should have been so over-prompt to acknowledge our national defeat. Throughout the whole course of our history that has been their consistent tradition, from the days of the Bourbon Restoration to those of the Versailles Assembly. Certainly, the confused issues of the Dreyfus affair did seem, for a moment, to have complicated matters by identifying patriotism with militarism. It is only natural that the deepest instincts of these men of the Right should once again have come out on top, and, on the whole, it is better that they should. But that the same men should, turn and turn about, have manifested the most fanatical anti-Germanism and a willingness to enter the continental system of Germany in the guise of vassals, that they should have defended Poincaré's diplomacy, yet damned the so-called 'war-mongering' of their political opponents, does call for thought. We can only assume that those of their leaders who were impelled by honest motives suffered from an almost incredible intellectual instability, and that among their faithful followers there was a no less shocking blindness to the antinomies of reason. I am perfectly well aware that the Germany of Hitler roused sympathies to which the Germany of Ebert could never have hoped to appeal, but that does not alter the fact that France has, fundamentally, remained the same. Those who seek, at any cost, to explain away such mental acrobatics could not, probably, do better than point out that the views held by those at the other end of the political scale were no less illogical. To refuse military credits, and then, twenty-four hours later, to call for 'guns for Spain'; to preach anti-patriotism, and then, in twelve months' time, to demand the formation of a 'French Front'; to shirk the obligations of military service, and to invite the masses to do the same—these inelegant zigzags mark only too clearly the curve traced before our wondering eyes by those who danced upon the tight-rope of Communism. I know perfectly well that beyond our frontier a brown-haired *Homo alpinus* of middle height, with a little red-headed cripple as his chief spokesman, managed to found a despotism on the myth of the Tall, Fair, Aryan Superman. But we French have always enjoyed the reputation—in the past, at least—of being solid, sensible, and logical. It does really seem that if ever our people are to be subjected to what Renan, after an earlier defeat, called an 'intellectual and moral reform', the first thing they will have to learn is that old axiom of classical logic—*A* is *A*: *B* is *B*: *A* is not *B*.

Naturally, much inquiry is necessary into, and a great deal can be said about, the underlying causes of these weaknesses. Our middle class, which, in spite of everything, remains the brain of the nation, was a great deal more addicted to serious studies when most of its members had independent means than it is to-day. The business man, the doctor, the lawyer, has to put in a hard day's work at his office. When he leaves it he is in no fit state, it would seem, for anything but amusement. Perhaps a better organization of the working day might, without diminishing the intensity of his labours, assure him a rather greater degree of leisure. But how about these amusements of his? Do they take an intellectual form? One thing is certain: they rarely have any connexion, even indirect, with his active life. For it is an ancient tradition among us, that intelligence should be enjoyed, like art, for its own sake, and should be kept carefully shut away from all possibility of practical application. We are a nation of great scientists, yet no technicians are less scientific than ours. We read, when we do read, with the object of acquiring culture. I have nothing against that. But it never seems to occur to us that culture can, and should, be a great help to us in our daily lives.

But what the French people really need is to be pupils once again in the school of true intellectual freedom. 'It is good that

151

heretics should exist.' Our military men were not alone in having lost sight of this wise maxim. About traditionalist opinion I will, for the moment, say nothing. It is as it is. But what are we to think of those who like to call themselves 'advanced'? I have a very great admiration for the works of Karl Marx. As a man he was, I fear, quite intolerable, and his philosophy is certainly a good deal less original than some people like to think. But never was there a more powerful analyst of the social problem. If ever those among our historians who are initiates of the newest cult of Social Science decide to set up a portrait gallery of their ancestors, the bearded bust of the old Rhineland prophet will take a foremost place in the chapel of their corporation. But is that any reason for establishing his teaching as the touchstone of all knowledge? There are admirable men of science who, though in the laboratory they believe in nothing but experimental research, will gaily write treatises on 'Marxist' physiology or chapters on 'Marxist' physics. What right have they, with those achievements to their credit, to point the finger of scorn at Hitlerian mathematics? Schools that formerly preached the doctrine of the mutability of economic forms have been known to excommunicate such ill-advised scholars as refuse to swear on the Gospel of the Master. As though theories born of the observation of European societies as they existed in the sixties of last century, and fed on such sociological knowledge as a scholar of that time possessed, could or should be regarded as Holy Writ in the year 1940!

Condorcet, a man impregnated with the powerful rationalism of the eighteenth century, showed a greater wisdom when, in his famous report on *Public Education*, he said: 'No class of our citizens should ever be led to regard either the French Constitution or even the Declaration of Rights as Tables of the Law sent down from Heaven, and to be treated only with adoration and unquestioning belief.'

I do not need anyone to whisper in my ear that the leaders of these various sects have been secretly far less faithful to their different orthodoxies than their acts and their public declarations might lead one to expect. I know all about that. But it does not alter the fact, does it, that in their horrible conclaves those very intellectual vices were much in evidence which have done us so much harm? To these was added a taste for certain ambiguities of expression, and a quite insufficient awareness of the truth that the world is always in a state of flux. In this matter of the men of the Left, as of the General Staff—for it often happens in the history of a nation that the bitterest adversaries breathe, unconsciously, the same intellectual atmosphere—Hitler was right. There is no getting away from it. Not the Hitler of the full-dress demagogic speeches, but the Hitler who once said to Rauschning when discussing this very question of Marxism: 'We, you and I, know that there isn't any final stability, but only a perpetual state of evolution. The future is an inexhaustible river of infinite possibilities whose source is a creation which is always being renewed.'

A university professor will be forgiven if he lays a great part of the responsibility for all this on education, and, himself an educator, does his best to expose, without undue beating about the bush, the defects of our teaching methods.

Our system of secondary education has been continuously oscillating, for a long time past, between an old-fashioned humanism which, aesthetically at least, has strong claims on its loyalty, and a taste—often excessive—for the new. But it is neither capable of preserving the aesthetic and moral standards of classical culture, nor of creating fresh ones to take their place. Consequently it has done little to develop the intellectual vitality of the nation. It lays upon its pupils the dead weight of examinations, and in this respect the universities are no better. It makes little room in its curriculum for those sciences which depend upon observation and might play so large a part in the training of visual concentration and the use of the grey matter of the

153

brain. It pays a great deal of attention to the physiology of plants—and quite rightly, but it almost entirely neglects field botany, and, in so doing, commits a grievous fault. In English schools the authorities make a great point of encouraging 'hobbies' (natural history, fossil-collecting, photography, and all sorts of odd pastimes). Our own pastors and masters, on the contrary, modestly avert their eyes from every kind of 'queer taste' or else leave such matters to the tender mercy of the Boy Scouts. Indeed, the success of the Scout movement probably shows more clearly than does anything else where the most yawning gaps are to be found in our national system of education. I know more than one boy who was an excellent performer in the classroom but never once so much as opened a serious book after he had left his secondary school. On the other hand, it is no rare thing to find that those who had the reputation with their masters of being dunces or near-dunces have since developed a real taste for the things of the mind. If such occurrences were occasional only, they would not be particularly significant. It is when they become multiplied that one begins uncomfortably to feel that 'something is wrong'.

Am I moved to say all this by the same sort of perversity that urges a lover to hurt the beloved? As an historian I am naturally inclined to be especially hard on the teaching of history. It is not only the Staff College that equips its pupils inadequately to face the test of action. I do not mean that the secondary schools can be accused with justice of neglecting the contemporary scene. On the contrary, they tend to give it an increasingly dominant place in the curriculum. But just because our teachers of history are inclined to focus their attention *only* on the present, or at most on the very recent past, they find the present more and more difficult to explain. They are like oceanographers who refuse to look up at the stars because they are too remote from the sea, and consequently are unable to discover the causes of the tides. I do not say that the past entirely governs the present, but I do maintain that we shall never satisfactorily understand the present unless we take the past into account. But there is still worse to come. Because our system of historical teaching deliberately cuts itself off from a wide field of vision and comparison, it can no longer impart to those whose minds it claims to form anything like a true sense of difference and change. Let me give an example of what I mean.

The policy which we pursued in the Rhineland after 1918 was based upon the picture of a Europe which no longer existed. It continued to treat as a living issue what was really a dead horse— German Separatism. Or again: our diplomats obstinately pinned their faith to the Hapsburgs—those faded ghosts fit only to adorn the 'keepsake' volumes on the tables of right-thinking conservatives. They were far more afraid of the Hohenzollerns than of Hitler. Any genuine theory of history would long ago have permitted those particular dead to bury their dead. Furthermore, those who drew up our school curricula had, almost all of them, a marked affection for all *recent* manifestation of national life, no matter how superficial, simply because they *were* recent, and easy to grasp. Consequently, they were obsessed by politics. They recoiled with a sense of outraged modesty from any suggestion of sociological analysis, and therefore failed to develop a taste for it in their pupils. No doubt some will say that I am expecting too much of boys who had only just reached matriculation standard. Against any such criticism I most vehemently protest. I do not believe that it is any more difficult to interest the young in the complexities of a technical problem or in the apparent oddities of a civilization which happens to be remote either in time or space, than it is to keep their minds fixed on the acts of politicians or the changes of governments. A text-book which sets out to explain how the July Monarchy substituted 'life peerages' for 'hereditary titles' is not, I suggest, a very useful work to put in the hands of junior students. They have more important things than that to learn, things more closely concerned with human values, better calculated to mould the malleable imagination of youth, and more instructive for the future citizens of France and of the world. What we need is that the windows should be thrown wide open and the atmosphere of our classrooms thoroughly aired. That will be the task of the rising generation. If we are to see a sounder intellectual training in the country at large, and a more efficient spirit in our military commanders, we must rely far more upon the young than upon the five academies, the great university authorities, and the Staff College.

Every conceivable sin is laid at the door of the political régime which governed France in the years before the war. I have only to look about me to feel convinced that the parliamentary system has too often favoured intrigue at the cost of intelligence and true loyalty. The men who govern us to-day were, for the most part, brought up in a land of mental bogs. If now they turn against the methods which made them what they are, that is only because they are sly old foxes who think the trick worth trying. The dishonest clerk who cracks the office safe is not likely to carry a bunch of skeleton keys about with him for all to see. He is far too frightened that someone cleverer than himself will pocket them and scoop the loot.

When the time for real reform at last comes round, when we can once again demand that we be led into the light of day, and that the political sects which have lost the nation's confidence be swept from the stage, we shall have to do better than set our feet in the tracks of the immediate past. The monstrously swollen assemblies which, in recent years, have claimed to rule us were one of the more absurd legacies of history. It mattered little that the States-General, convened to pronounce a simple 'Yes' or 'No', should have a membership of hundreds. But a chamber whose function it is to run the country must become chaotic once it has allowed itself to degenerate into a mob. It is, indeed, a question whether a chamber which was designed merely to sanction and control, *can* govern. Our party machinery had already begun to give off the smell of a dry-rot which it had acquired in small cafés and obscure back rooms. It could not even offer the excuse that it was strong, because at the first breath of despotism it collapsed like a house of cards. Imprisoned in doctrines which they knew to be outmoded, of programmes which they had long abandoned as signposts to practical politics, the great parties served as sham rallying-points for men who, on all the major problems of the moment—as was only too obvious after Munich—held utterly opposed views. They declared themselves to be at odds with others whose members thought, in fact, precisely as they did. More often than not they failed even to determine who was to wield the power. They served merely as spring-boards for clever careerists who spent their time knocking one another off the top of the political structure.

It was entirely owing to our ministers and our assemblies that we were so ill prepared for war. Of that there can be not the slightest doubt. Not, it is true, that the High Command did much to help them. But nothing shed a cruder light on the spinelessness of Government than its capitulation to the technicians. In 1915 a succession of Parliamentary Commissions did more to provide us with heavy artillery than did all the artillerymen put together. Why did not their successors do more, and do it quicker, in the matter of aeroplanes and tanks? The history of the Ministry of Munitions reads like a lesson in unreason. It is incredible that we should have had to wait until the war was several months old before it was even set up, and then only as a makeshift organization. It should have been ready to start work, with a staff already picked and prepared, on the very day that mobilization was ordered. Only very exceptionally did Parliament ever refuse credits if the specialists demanded them with sufficient firmness, but it lacked the power to compel their proper use. It could, had it so wished, have put its hand in the elector's pocket, but it was afraid of irritating him. Its dislike of imposing on reservists the necessary period of field-training undermined the whole principle of the nation in arms. True, the routine of the barrack-square—not the best way of utilizing these periods of instruction—did at least set that particular ball rolling, but that is not saying much. More than once the leaders of the Government found themselves driven to ask for extraordinary powers—which was tantamount to admitting that the constitutional machinery was getting rusty. It would have been far better to redesign the machine while there was yet time. Those extraordinary powers were the line of least resistance, though nobody seems to have realized that they merely served to reinforce the existing practices of government and did nothing towards reforming them. Spoiled by a long familiarity with the lobbies, our political leaders imagined that they were gleaning information when all they were doing was to collect gossip from chance acquaintances. All problems, of the world as well as of the nation, appeared to them in the light of personal rivalries.

That the system suffered from weaknesses there can be no denying; but it was not so inherently vicious as has sometimes been argued. Many of the crimes of which it has been accused were, I should say, purely imaginary. It is often said that party, and, in particular, anti-clerical, passions disorganized the armed forces. I can bear witness from my own experience that at Bohain General Blanchard went to Mass every Sunday. To assume that he had waited until war broke out to do so would be to level a gratuitous insult at his civic courage. It was right and proper that he, as a believer, should publicly perform his religious duties. The unbeliever who held such acts against him showed himself to be a fool or a boor. But I see no reason to maintain that those religious convictions, loyally adhered to, stood in the way of his being given an army by a succession of so-called Left-Wing governments, or of his leading it to defeat.

Did those parliaments of ours, if it comes to that, or the

ministries born of them, ever really concentrate the government of the country in their own hands? Earlier systems had left a legacy of public corporations which the politicians never really succeeded in controlling. No doubt party considerations did to some extent weigh in the appointment of the heads of these bodies, and, as the winds of the moment blew, so did personalities change—not always with the happiest results. But, fundamentally, these great organizations were self-governing, and the men who formed their rank and file always remained, roughly, of the same type. The École des Sciences Politiques, for instance, was always the spiritual home of scions of rich and powerful families. Its graduates filled the embassies, the Treasury, the Council of State, and the Public Audit Office. The École Polytechnique, with its curious power of leaving an indelible and recognizable imprint on the young men who had passed through it, did far more than supply recruits for the general staffs of industry. It unlocked the door to a career in public engineering, where promotion had almost the automatic precision of a well-oiled machine. The universities, through the medium of a complex arrangement of councils and committees, filled any vacancies there might be in their teaching-staffs by a system of co-option which was not without its dangers when the need for new blood arose, and could offer to their successful students guarantees of permanent employment which the system at present in force has—provisionally, it is said—abolished. The Institute of France, entrenched in its wealth and in that prestige which the glitter of a title can always impose even on those who pass for being philosophically minded, still retains, for good or ill, the full dignity of its intellectual pre-eminence. If the Academy might occasionally be influenced in its elections by political considerations, it can scarcely be maintained that these have been of a Left-Wing kind. 'I know of only three citadels of Conservatism,' said Paul Bourget on one occasion, 'the House of Lords, the German General Staff, and the French Academy.'

Was the régime right or wrong in the consideration it habitually showed to these ancient corporations? The subject might be discussed endlessly. Some will uphold them in the interests of stability and in recognition of an honourable tradition. Others, with whom, I confess, my own sympathies lie, will argue against them on grounds of bureaucratic tendencies, routine mentality, and professional arrogance. But there are certainly two things for which a heavy responsibility lay at their door.

They raised a clamorous outcry when a Popular Front Government, in an effort to break down the monopoly held by the École des Sciences Politiques, presumed to establish a School of Administration. Not that the project was a particularly good one. It would have been very much better to throw open an administrative career to all by means of a system of public scholarships, and to let candidates be prepared by the universities along those cultural lines which have served the English civil service so well. But, for all that, the underlying idea was sound. Whatever the complexion of its government, a country is bound to suffer if the *instruments* of power are hostile to the spirit which obtains in the various branches of its public institutions. A monarchy needs a personnel composed of monarchists. A democracy becomes hopelessly weak, and the general good suffers accordingly, if its higher officials, bred up to despise it, and necessarily drawn from those very classes the dominance of which it is pledged to destroy, serve it only half-heartedly.

The other point which can justly be brought against them is this. The system of co-option which, whether officially or unofficially, was the rule in almost all the great public corporations, tended to give much too prominent a place to age. As in the Army, promotion—with very few exceptions—was, generally speaking, slow, and the old men at the top, even when they did show willingness to help their juniors up the ladder, were inclined to pick their men from among those who had shown themselves to be model pupils—almost excessively model. We judge revolutions to be admirable or hateful according as their principles are or are not our own. All of them, however, have one supreme virtue which is inseparable from the vigour out of which they grow: they do thrust the young into positions of prominence. I detest Nazism, but, like the French Revolution, with which one should blush to compare it, it did put at the head, both of its armed forces and of its Government, men who, because their brains were fresh and had not been formed in the routine of the schools, were capable of understanding 'the surprising and the new'. All we had to set against them was a set of bald-pates and youngish dotards.

But however powerful the resistance offered by a Government's machinery may be, the *system* is the creation of the society which is said to be governed by it. Sometimes the engine may run away with the driver, but, as a rule, it will give good service if it is properly handled. I find it difficult not to laugh when I hear certain business men of my acquaintance inveighing against the venality of the Press just after they have managed to get some article 'planted' (in return for good hard cash) on one of our more respectable dailies, or when they have commissioned a former minister to write a book which will bolster up their own petty interests, fulminating against 'Parliamentary men of straw'! Who most deserves to be hanged, the corrupted or the corrupter? Our rich *bourgeois* like nothing better than to grumble at the teaching profession. In the days when they controlled the money-bags much more completely than they do to-day, they had it in their power to provide in the budget for a reasonable scale of pay for schoolmasters. What, in fact, they did was to give those who were entrusted with the education of their sons far less than they would have dreamed of giving to their servants. The reputation for avarice has done the French people an infinity of harm: and it is this provincial attitude of mind that has been responsible.

But what, more than anything else, has injured our machinery of State, and, literally, stopped it from working, is that major lack of understanding which lies like a blight over the minds of almost all Frenchmen.

It is a good thing, and a sign of health, that those in a free country who represent contrasted social theories should freely air their differences. Society to-day being what it is, class interests are bound to be at odds. Antagonisms there must be, and it is well that they should be recognized. It is only when this state of social friction ceases to be regarded as normal and legitimate that the country as a whole begins to suffer.

More than once in the course of this book I have made use of the word *bourgeoisie*—not without a qualm of conscience. The sciences which have human beings as their subject are, at best, but empirical, and their pursuit is made more than ever difficult when they are cluttered up with words which have become so debased by long use that their meaning has ceased to be clear. The realities which they express are too complex; the language which expresses them too fluid. That, however, is beyond our power to alter. Until some better means of communication than that of language has been evolved, we must resign ourselves to using the only vocabulary which the imperfections of our tongue have made available. But it can be used successfully only if we define our terms. Let me say, then, that, when speaking of Frenchmen I employ the term *bourgeois*, I mean someone who is not dependent for his livelihood on the work of his hands; whose income, irrespective of its source and of its size (for it may vary considerably from individual to individual), permits him to live in easy circumstances, and gives him a sense of security such as no mere wage-earner can ever know in his own hazardous existence; whose education, enjoyed from birth, if his family happens to be an old-established one, or gained in the course of an exceptional rise in the social scale, is richer in texture, better in quality, and more pretentious in kind than the minimum cultural training enjoyed by the ordinary man in the street. Finally, the *bourgeois* is a man who believes that he belongs to a class which is marked out for leadership in the country's affairs, and, by a thousand little details of dress, language, and good manners, shows more or less instinctively that he is one of a very special group and enjoys a high degree of prestige in the eyes of less fortunate mortals.

Now, the *bourgeoisie,* thus defined, was not feeling any too happy in pre-war France. The economic changes which it was the fashion to lay at the door of the last world catastrophe, though some of them had other causes, were in process of sapping the foundations of those solid, unadventurous fortunes which had existed in earlier days when an income from investments had formed the sole resource of many families, and was the goal of many others whose members were just beginning to climb the ladder of success. In the world brought into existence by the first war, this kind of livelihood was beginning to melt away in the hands of its astonished possessors. The workers were setting their faces stubbornly against all attempts to reduce wages, with the result that after each recurrent crisis, profits and dividends alike grew smaller. The spread of industry in new countries which showed an increasing tendency to become self-sufficient was producing an ever-worsening condition of anaemia in the capitalistic system not only of France but of Europe generally. The aggressive mood of the new-comers to the social scene was already threatening the economic and political power of a group which had long been accustomed to command, and had conveniently come to terms with the institutions of a democracy to which many of its members had even sworn allegiance. As usually happens, custom had lagged behind fact. The franchise had been widened to include workers on the land and in the factories, but the exercise of the vote had not as yet seriously shaken the traditional position of superiority enjoyed, outside the capital, by the bigwigs of the middle class. Indeed, to some extent it benefited them, because they were able, partially at least, to eliminate from the great offices of state their old adversaries of the great noble and near-noble families. Untouched by aristocratic arrogance, their outlook on life was genuinely humanistic, and it drew strength from a democratic system so long as that system did not strike at them through their pockets or undermine the solid structure of their very real, though modest, prestige. But a day soon came when the voters of the lowest category, encouraged in their demands by the economic tragedy of the times, began to make their voices heard. And what those voices now expressed was something that was a great deal more dangerous than it had formerly been. Old resentments drew fresh vigour from an exacerbated sense of inequality. The *bourgeois*, forced to realize that he had got to work a good deal harder than he had done in the past, got the idea that the 'masses', whose labour was, in the last analysis, the source of his own profits, were working less—which was true, and even less than he was—which was not, perhaps, equally true, and certainly did not take into account the difference in degree of human fatigue. He grew indignant at the thought that the manual worker had now enough free time to enable him to go to the cinema like his boss. The workers' attitude to money, born of a long past of insecurity which had firmly fixed in their minds the conviction that it was useless to look ahead, and that the morrow could be left to take care of itself, offended his inborn respect for the virtue of saving. Even the most charitable-minded sought in vain among the crowds parading with clenched fists raised, and demanding their rights with a violence which, in fact, was no more than a rather crude expression of honest frankness, the 'respectable poor' who had peopled with such deferential charm the novels of Madame de Ségur. The value of discipline, of docile good-nature, of a ready acceptance of social differences by the less fortunate, had formed the basis of their timid and unadventurous education. And now it looked as though all these things were to be swept away for good and all. With them, they felt, would go something far more valuable, that sense of the common weal which, little though the comfortably off might think it, does demand a greater degree of sacrifice from the poor than from the rich.

Because, for all these reasons, the members of the *bourgeoisie* had grown anxious and discontented, they now began to show signs of bitterness. They might, had they looked a little closer, have reached a better understanding of the 'People' from whom they were themselves sprung, and with whom they had more than one deep affinity. But because they were unused to making the mental effort which social analysis demands, they preferred to condemn out of hand. It would be difficult to exaggerate the sense of shock felt by the comfortable classes, and even by men who had a reputation for liberal-mindedness, at the coming of the Popular Front in 1936. All those who had a few pennies to bless themselves with smelled the rising wind of disaster, and the good housewife was, if anything, more terrified than her husband. It is the fashion to-day to say that the Jews were behind the Left-Wing movement. Poor Synagogue—always fated to act as scapegoat! I know, from what I saw with my own eyes, that it trembled even more violently than the Church. The same held true of the non-Catholic congregations. 'The old Protestant employer's a thing of the past'—I heard a writer say who had been brought up in Nonconformist circles. 'At one time no one could have been more whole-heartedly concerned for the well-being of his people than he was, but now he is among the most rancorous of their critics.' A deep fissure was opening almost before our eyes in the fabric of French social life. The country was splitting into two opposed groups.

It is no part of my intention to enter the lists as a champion of the Popular Front governments. They are dead now, and those who for a moment put their faith in them may, perhaps, be allowed to cast a handful of dust in pious memory on their graves. More than this they do not deserve. They fell without glory, and what makes it worse is that their adversaries had little to do with their overthrow. Events outstripped them, but even that is not the whole story. The movement failed mainly because of the follies of its supporters, or of those who claimed to be its supporters. Still, the attitude of the greater part of middle-class opinion was inexcusable. It grumbled with stupid mulishness at everything that was done, whether good or bad. One decent fellow of my acquaintance obstinately refused to set his foot inside the Exposition Universelle. He liked looking at beautiful things, and it offered for his enjoyment an incomparable display of the glories of French art. But that made not the slightest difference. It was enough for him that a detested minister had officiated at the opening ceremony! It was said that the demands of organized labour had, at one moment, raised doubts as to its being ready in time, and that was enough to put it outside the pale. And what an outcry there was when the authorities began to talk about the organization of leisure! The idea was greeted with mockery, and attempts were even made to bring it to nothing. Yet the very people who took that attitude then are now prepared to extol to the skies similar efforts, made more or less seriously, though under a different name, by régimes after their own hearts.

But whatever the faults of which the movement may have been guilty, there was in that striving of the masses to make a juster world a touching eagerness and sincerity which ought not to have been without effect on any man animated by ordinary human feelings. But how many employers of my acquaintance have I ever found capable of understanding, for instance, what nobility may lie behind a 'sympathetic' strike, no matter how unreasonable? 'It isn't', they say, 'as though the men were striking for their *own* wages.' There are two categories of Frenchmen who will never really grasp the significance of French history: those who refuse to thrill to the Consecration of our

Kings at Rheims, and those who can read unmoved the account of the Festival of Federation. I do not care what may be the colour of their politics to-day: such a lack of response to the noblest uprushes of national enthusiasm is enough to condemn them. In the Popular Front—the *real* Popular Front of the masses, not the one exploited by the politicians—something lived again of the spirit that had moved men's hearts on the Champ-de-Mars under the hot sun of 14 July 1790. Unfortunately, the men whose ancestors pledged their faith on the Altar of the Nation have lost contact with the profound realities of national greatness. It is no accident that our régime, in spite of all its democratic trappings, has never been able to create for the people of France festivals capable of sounding a note to the ears of all the world. We have left it to Hitler to revive the paeans of the Ancient World. When I was with the First Army I saw a good deal of certain officers who had been given the task of raising the morale of the troops. The High Command had chosen for this duty a banker who was a Parisian to his finger-tips, and an industrialist from the north. They thought that the best way of slipping a few 'home truths' into the trench newspapers was to give them a plentiful coating of rather crude humour. As to the field theatres, well, the more they concentrated on smutty farces, the better pleased the authorities were. The *bourgeoisie* lived completely separated from the people. Its members made no attempt to reach that understanding which might have led to sympathy. Turn and turn about, either they refused to take the masses seriously, or they trembled before their implied threat. What they did not realize was that, by so doing, they were separating themselves effectively from France.

As a result of attacking the régime, these same *bourgeois* proceeded, naturally, to condemn the nation which had produced it. Driven to despair of their own future, they ended by despairing of their country. If anyone be tempted to say that I exaggerate, let him re-read the newspapers on which, a few years ago, the middle classes lived, and whose outlook they dictated. He will find the experience edifying. At the time when Belgium had just rejected the offer of an alliance in favour of a neutrality which unhappily turned out to be fallacious, a friend of mine in Brussels said: 'You've no idea of the amount of damage done to the French cause by your great Weeklies. They declare in every issue that France, as a nation, is in an advanced stage of putrescence. Well, I'm afraid we believe 'em. How can you expect us not to?' We ourselves believed them only too well. Many men of what might still claim to be our ruling classes, since from them were drawn our leaders of industry, our senior civil servants, the majority of our reserve officers, set off for the war haunted by these gloomy prognostications. They were taking their orders from a political set-up which they held to be hopelessly corrupt. They were defending a country which they did not seriously think could offer any genuine resistance. The soldiers under their command were the sons of that 'People' which they were only too glad to regard as degenerate. No matter how high their own courage, no matter how resolute their own patriotism, it can hardly be maintained that this was the best intellectual preparation for men who would be called upon to fight 'to the last quarter of an hour'.

Now, those who provided the personnel for the various military staffs were only too ready to share these jaundiced points of view. I do not mean that they were all to the same extent contaminated. It was by no means true that *all* regular officers, even those in the most senior positions, necessarily belonged to the world of hereditary wealth. More than one, on the contrary, hailed from a social level which was little, if at all, removed from that of the great mass of his countrymen. By the nature of their calling, and as a point of honour, they were for the most part strangers to the petty outlook of the tradesman. The future of capitalism—supposing that they ever had time to think about such things—would not have caused them any

particular concern, and most of them would have been left unmoved by the prospect of a redistribution of the national wealth.
Almost all of them were men with a strong sense of duty, fervent
patriots, and very conscious that they were soldiers of France.
The idea that they might be regarded as the mercenaries of
certain private interests, or of any one class, would have brought
a blush of shame to their cheeks. But what did they know of
social realities? Education, the spirit of caste, tradition, had all
combined to build around them a wall of ignorance and error.
Their thoughts were simple. The 'Left' meant for them 'anti-
militarism', free thought, and a hatred of that authority which,
as everyone knows, is the main source of an army's strength.
About Socialists they had long known all there was to know.
They equated the word with the 'bad' soldier, the man who
always has a grouse, and, horror of horrors, sometimes com-
municates his grievances to the Press. Anyone who had dealings
with 'Socialists' became automatically suspect. Even Roosevelt
had something of the 'Bolshie' about him (I actually heard that
said once by a highly placed staff officer). They were not, as a
whole, intellectually curious, and they had been trained from
boyhood to flee from heresy as from the plague. This brief and
simple orthodoxy was admirably suited to their needs. They
never made the slightest attempt to acquire information. Among
the newspapers which lay on our anteroom table, *Le Temps* was,
by comparison with its neighbours, a 'red rag'. And so it came
about that a whole group of young leaders, recruited from among
the most intelligent representatives of the nation, never opened
a daily paper which reflected, even in the smallest degree, the
opinions professed, rightly or wrongly, by the majority of
Frenchmen.

There is no getting away from the fact that we, the teachers,
were largely to blame for this state of affairs. I have long felt
it to be deplorable that men whose proud boast it was in
recent years that they stood for all that was most liberal, most

disinterested, and most humanly progressive, in our country, should have been guilty of the serious charge of having made no effort whatever to touch the understanding of a professional body which enshrined such high moral values. Their failure to do so dates, I think, from the Dreyfus affair, and the original responsibility does not rest on the shoulders of those who, at that time, were on our side of the barricades. But that is no excuse for what has happened since. Many a time I have said to myself, as I saw my companions drinking in like harmless milk the poisonous brew compacted of stupidity and hatred which certain squalid sheets continued to dispense even during the war: 'What a shame it is that such fine fellows should be so ill informed: what a crying scandal that no one has ever really tried to enlighten them.'

The fact remains that we are now in a position to measure up the results. Ill informed about the infinite resources of a people that has remained far healthier than they, as the result of poisonous teaching, have been inclined to believe; rendered incapable by inherited contempt and by the limited routine of their training to call in time upon its inexhaustible reserves of strength, our leaders not only let themselves be beaten, but too soon decided that it was perfectly natural that they should be beaten. By laying down their arms before there was any real necessity for them to do so, they have assured the triumph of a faction. Some of them, to be sure, strove hard, by backing the *coup d'état*, to disguise their fault. But others there were, in the High Command and in almost every rank of the Army, who were very far from pursuing any such selfish design. They accepted the disaster, but with rage in their hearts. However that may be, they did accept it, and long before they need have done. They were ready to find consolation in the thought that beneath the ruins of France a shameful régime might be crushed to death, and that if they yielded it was to a punishment meted out by Destiny to a guilty nation.

The generation to which I belong has a bad conscience. It is true that we emerged from the last war desperately tired, and that after four years not only of fighting, but of mental laziness, we were only too anxious to get back to our proper employments and take up the tools that we had left to rust upon the benches. So behindhand were we with our work that we set ourselves to bolt it down in indigestible mouthfuls. That is our excuse. But I have long ceased to believe that it can wash us clean of guilt.

Many of us realized at a very early stage the nature of the abyss into which the diplomacy of Versailles and the Ruhr was threatening to plunge us. We knew perfectly well that it would have the double result of embroiling us with our former Allies and of keeping open and bleeding our ancient quarrel with an enemy whom we had just, but only just, defeated. We were not ignorant of the potentialities of power latent in both Germany and Britain. The same, or roughly the same, men whom we have heard to-day preaching, before the last hour had struck, the gloomy wisdom of Louis XVIII, were then urging us on to ape the grandiloquent arrogance of Louis XIV. We were not such fools as to believe that in a France impoverished, relatively undermanned, and capable of realizing only a very small industrial potential, a policy of the kind they contemplated was advisable— if, indeed, it would have been so at any time. Not being prophets we did not foresee the advent of the Nazis. But we did foresee that, in some form or other, though its precise nature was hidden from us, a German revival *would* come, that it would be embittered by rancorous memories to which our foolish ineptitude was daily adding, and that its explosion would be terrible. Had anyone asked us how we thought a second war would end we should, I doubt not, have answered that we hoped it would end in victory. But we should have been perfectly clear in our own minds that if the terrible storm broke again there was grave danger that the whole of European civilization might well suffer irremediable shipwreck. We did realize that in the Germany of that time there were signs, however timid, of a new spirit of goodwill, of an attitude that was frankly pacific and honestly liberal. The only thing wanting was a gesture of encouragement on the part of our political leaders. We knew all that, and yet, from laziness, from cowardice, we let things take their course. We feared the opposition of the mob, the sarcasm of our friends, the ignorant mistrust of our masters. We dared not stand up in public and be the voice crying in the wilderness. It might have been just that, but at least we should have had the consolation of knowing that, whatever the outcome of its message, it had at least spoken aloud the faith that was in us. We preferred to lock ourselves into the fear-haunted tranquillity of our studies. May the young men forgive us the blood that is red upon our hands!

All, or almost all, these things had long been whispered among intimate friends: the weakness that was slowly undermining the robust health of the nation; the intellectual lethargy of our ruling classes, and their bitter grievances; the illogical propaganda which was providing so adulterate but so heady a draught for our workers; the dominance of age, and the unrest in the Army. But how many had the courage to speak their thoughts aloud? I know well enough that we lacked the partisan spirit, and that is something of which we need not be ashamed. Those of us—and they were the exceptions—who let themselves be caught up in one or other of the political parties almost always ended by being its prisoners rather than its guides. It was not to work on electoral committees that our duty should have urged us. We had tongues and brains in our heads and pens in our hands. But we were all of us either specialists in the social sciences or workers in scientific laboratories, and maybe the very disciplines of those employments kept us, by a sort of fatalism, from embarking on individual action. We had grown used to seeing great impersonal forces at work in society as in nature. In the vast drag of these submarine swells, so cosmic as to seem

irresistible, of what avail were the petty struggles of a few ship-
wrecked sailors? To think otherwise would have been to falsify
history. Among all the characteristics that mark the rise and fall
of civilizations, I know of none that is more significant than the
gradual movement of the collective mind towards self-conscious-
ness. In that fact lies the key to many of the contrasts that show,
however crudely, as between the societies of the past and those
of to-day. Juridical changes, as soon as they grow large enough
to be noted, look very different from what they would have done
had the movement remained purely instinctive.

The movements of the Stock Exchange vary according as the
fluctuation of current prices are or are not known to the aggregate
of shareholders. But of what is the general mind composed if not
of a multitude of individual minds which continually act and
react upon one another? For a man to form a clear idea of the
needs of society and to make an effort to spread his views
widely is to introduce a grain of leaven into the general mentality.
By so doing he gives himself a chance to modify it to some small
extent, and, consequently, to bring some influence to bear upon
the course of events which, in the last analysis, are dictated by
human psychology. The real trouble with us professors was that
we were absorbed in our day-to-day tasks. Most of us can say
with some justice that we were good workmen. Is it equally
true to say that we were good citizens?

In thus parading my remorse for things left undone, I am
actuated by no sense of gloomy pleasure. I have never learned
from experience that a sin is any the less heavy to bear because it
has been confessed. No, I am thinking of those who will read
these words, of my sons certainly, of others perhaps, and they
may be of a younger generation. I ask them to reflect on the
faults of their elders. It matters little whether they judge them
with ruthless severity, or pay them the rather contemptuous and
grudging tribute of that amused indulgence which adolescents
are prepared to accord to age. The important thing is that they

should realize what those faults were, so that they may be in a position to avoid them when their turn comes.

We find ourselves to-day in this appalling situation—that the fate of France no longer depends upon the French. Since that moment when the weapons which we held with too indeterminate a grasp fell from our hands, the future of our country and of our civilization has become the stake in a struggle of which we, for the most part, are only the rather humiliated spectators. What will become of us if, by some hideous mischance, Great Britain is in turn defeated? Our recovery as a nation will, it is quite certain, be long retarded. But *only* retarded, of that I am sure. The deep-seated vitality of our people is intact, and, sooner or later, will show signs of recovery. That of nazified Germany, on the contrary, cannot endure indefinitely the increasing strain which its masters see fit to impose upon it. Foreign systems brought into France in the 'baggage wagons of the enemy' have, on more than one occasion, lasted for a limited time. But the detestation of a proud nation has always, in the long run, proved too strong, and, sooner or later, sentence has been pronounced. Already we feel the iron of occupation eating more cruelly into our flesh. The seeming good-nature of the early days no longer deceives anybody. We have but to see Hitlerism in its day-to-day manifestations to condemn it. But I would so much rather look forward to an eventual British victory! I cannot tell when the hour will sound when, thanks to our Allies, we can once more control our own destiny. But when it does sound, shall we see scraps and corners of our territory liberate themselves successively from the enemy? Shall we see wave after wave of volunteer armies spring into being all agog to answer to the renewed appeal of 'The Country in Danger'? Maybe some tiny autonomous government will suddenly appear in some remote district and spread like a patch of oil. It may be, on the other hand, that a great surge of national feeling will develop swiftly. An elderly historian likes to arrange patterns with these pictures of a possible future, though imperfect knowledge makes it impossible for him to choose between them. My only hope, and I make no bones about it, is that when the moment comes we shall have enough blood left to shed, even though it be the blood of those who are dear to us (I say nothing of my own, to which I attach no importance). For there can be no salvation where there is not some sacrifice, and no national liberty in the fullest sense unless we have ourselves worked to bring it about.

The duty of reconstructing our country will not fall on the shoulders of my generation. France in defeat will be seen to have had a Government of old men. That is but natural. France of the new springtime must be the creation of the young. As compared with their elders of the last war, they will have one sad privilege: they will not have to guard against the lethargy bred of victory. Whatever form the final triumph may take, it will be many years before the stain of 1940 can be effaced. It may be a good thing that these young people will have to work in a white heat of rage. It would be impertinent on my part to outline a programme for them. They will search for the laws of the future in the intimacy of their heads and of their hearts. The map of the future will be drawn as a result of the lessons they have learned. All I beg of them is that they shall avoid the dry inhumanity of systems which, from rancour or from pride, set themselves to rule the mass of their countrymen without providing them with adequate instruction, without being in true communion with them. Our people deserve to be trusted, to be taken into the confidence of their leaders. I hope, too, that though they may do new things, many new things, they will not break the links that bind us to our authentic heritage, which is not at all, or, at least, not wholly, what some self-styled apostles of tradition have imagined it to be. On one occasion Hitler said to Rauschning: 'It is very much better to bank on the vices of men than on their virtues. The French Revolution appealed to virtue. We shall be better advised to do the contrary.' A

175

A Frenchman Examines his Conscience

Frenchman, that is to say, a civilized man—for the two are identical—will be forgiven if he substitute for this teaching that of the Revolution and of Montesquieu: 'A State founded on the People needs a mainspring: and that mainspring is virtue.' What matter if the task is thereby made more difficult—as it will be? A free people in pursuit of noble ends runs a double risk. But are soldiers on the field of battle to be warned against the spirit of adventure?

GUÉRET-FOUGÈRES (CREUSE)
  July–September 1940

THE TESTAMENTARY INSTRUCTIONS OF
MARC BLOCH[1]

WHEN death comes to me, whether in France or abroad, I leave it to my dear wife or, failing her, to my children, to arrange for such burial as may seem best to them. I wish the ceremony to be a civil one only. The members of my family know that I could accept no other kind. But when the moment comes I should like some friend to take upon himself the task of reading the following words, either in the mortuary or at the graveside.

I have not asked to have read above my body those Jewish prayers to the cadence of which so many of my ancestors, including my father, were laid to rest. All my life I have striven to achieve complete sincerity in word and thought. I hold that any compromise with untruth, no matter what the pretext, is the mark of a human soul's ultimate corruption. Following in this a far greater man than I could ever hope to be, I could wish for no better epitaph than these simple words:—DILEXIT VERITATEM. That is why I find it impossible, at this moment of my last farewell, when, if ever, a man should be true to himself, to authorize any use of those formulae of an orthodoxy to the beliefs of which I have ever refused to subscribe.

But I should hate to think that anyone might read into this statement of personal integrity even the remotest approximation to a coward's denial. I am prepared, therefore, if necessary, to affirm here, in the face of death, that I was born a Jew: that I have never denied it, nor ever been tempted to do so. In a world assailed by the most appalling barbarism, is not that generous tradition of the Hebrew

[1] The text here printed was given by Marc Bloch to his family at the time when he was engaged in clandestine activities. There can be few finer examples of beauty of mind expressed in such beauty of handwriting.

Four years after writing the 'Statement of the Evidence' contained in the preceding pages, and one year after committing these last wishes, in which he sums up all he had to say, with diamond-like precision, Marc Bloch fell to the bullets of a Nazi firing-squad.

Prophets, which Christianity at its highest and noblest took over and expanded, one of the best justifications we can have for living, believing, and fighting? A stranger to all credal dogmas, as to all pretended community of life and spirit based on race, I have, through life, felt that I was above all, and quite simply, a Frenchman. A family tradition, already of long date, has bound me firmly to my country. I have found nourishment in her spiritual heritage and in her history. I can, indeed, think of no other land whose air I could have breathed with such a sense of ease and freedom. I have loved her greatly, and served her with all my strength. I have never found that the fact of being a Jew has at all hindered these sentiments. Though I have fought in two wars, it has not fallen to my lot to die for France. But I can, at least, in all sincerity, declare that I die now, as I have lived, a good Frenchman.

When these words have been spoken, the same friend shall, if the text can be obtained, read the citations which I received for service in the field.